About the Author:

Tom Hollins is an English specialist and consultant in Staffordshire and Derbyshire. He works for many top educational companies to help write content and to mark work in A-Level English Language. He attained at A* at A-Level, scoring in the top 0.5% of the country and went on to continue his study of English at University.

He wanted to help students with their study of English at A-Level and so decided to produce this book. He also runs a blog entitled 'The Lexical Spectacle'. You can also find him on Twitter: @TheLexmeme.

Dedications and thanks:

I would like to dedicate this book to Karen Bell and Rachel Hunt. Without them, I wouldn't be writing this. They inspired my love and passion for the English Language and for that, I am always and forever grateful.

I would like to thank the following:

- Ethan Lee – for allowing me to use your Original Writing in the book. I owe you a coffee.
- Laura Robinson, Melissa Coulton and Richard Young – for being my brilliant proof-readers.

Table of Contents

How to use this book

In order to avoid copyright infringement, this book will not use any copyrighted material like articles or texts, however, there is a companion to this book available for FREE, if you have purchased this book. Simply email: TheLexicalSpectacle@gmail.com and I will email you a comprehensive list of links to articles and texts which you can use to help you.

This book covers the entire specification for AQA A-Level English Language. Throughout the book, you will find content, theory, exam advice, writing frames, essay plans and model essays.

> Things with black boxes round them are writing frames for you to use in your answers.

Things with dashed-line boxes around them are model answers.

There is also a glossary at the end of the book where you can look up any terms you are unsure of.

The following code will be used throughout the book:
- /x/ - a phoneme – this represents a sound.
- <x> - a grapheme – this represents a letter.

Please note, this book is not endorsed by or affiliated with AQA. The advice in this book is based on my personal experience with the exams and mark schemes. As with all revision guides, it does not guarantee you a grade. All exam answers, essay plans and mock questions have been generated by me and have not been approved by AQA. The model answers supplied obviously do not provide the only possible structure or solution to the answer. No content which AQA have published has been knowingly reproduced in this guide and any content which is found to be a replication of any AQA content will be removed. Please refer to the AQA website for all official guidance.

Overview of Assessment

Your English Language A-Level is assessed via three different assessments:
1. EXAM: Language, The Individual and Society – 100 marks – 40% weighting
2. EXAM: Language Diversity and Change – 100 marks – 40% weighting
3. NON-EXAM ASSESSMENT: Language in Action – 100 marks – 20% weighting

Each exam component assesses different skills, but all of them assess your ability to write in order to convey your ideas. It's important to spend time practising writing and finding your style.

There are five assessment objectives which all questions and assessments in English Language are marked against; you should try to memorise these:

AO1: Apply appropriate methods of language analysis, using associated terminology and coherent written expression.

AO2: Demonstrate critical understanding of concepts and issues relevant to language use.

AO3: Analyse and evaluate how contextual factors and language features are associated with the construction of meaning.

AO4: Explore connections across texts, informed by linguistic concepts and methods.

AO5: Demonstrate expertise and creativity in the use of English to communicate in different ways.

As you read through this guide, each section is clearly labelled in terms of the assessment objectives which are being assessed. These are not always equally important and some are worth more marks than others. In a very simplified way:

AO1 – terminology
AO2 – theory
AO3 – context
AO4 – links and connections
AO5 – creativity

OVERVIEW OF ASSESSMENT		
Paper 1: Language, the Individual and Society. 100 marks, 40% of the A-Level.	Paper 2: Language Diversity and Change. 100 marks, 40% of the A-Level.	Non-Exam Assessment: Language in Action. 100 marks, 20% of the A-Level.
Question 1 - Analyse how Text A uses language to create meanings and representations. (MODERN TEXT) AO1: 10 marks, AO3: 15 marks. Total - 25 marks.	EITHER Question 1 - Language diversity. Evaluate the idea that... (NO DATA GIVEN) AO1: 10 marks, AO2: 20 marks. Total - 30 marks.	Original Writing. A piece of writing which is informative, narrative or persuasive. Assesses AO5 for 25 marks.

A commentary piece in which you explain the creative process in which the writing was produced. Including reference to a style model. Marked out of all assessment objectives for a total of 25.

50 marks total. |
| Question 2 - Analyse how Text B uses language to create meanings and representations. (HISTORICAL TEXT) AO1: 10 marks, AO3: 15 marks. Total - 25 marks. | OR Question 2 - Language change. Evaluate the idea that... (NO DATA GIVEN) AO1: 10 marks, AO2: 20 marks. Total - 30 marks. | |
| Question 3 - Explore the similarities and differences in the ways that Text A and Text B use language. AO4: 20 marks (informed by AO1 and AO3, but no explicit marks). | Question 3 - Analyse how language is used in Text A and Text B to present views about... AO1: 10 marks, AO3: 15 marks, AO4: 15 marks. Total - 40 marks. | Language investigation.

An in-depth investigation into an area of language of your choice.

The piece should contain:
1. Introduction
2. Methodology
3. Analysis
4. Conclusion

AO1: 15 marks, AO2: 15 marks, AO3: 20 marks.
50 marks. |
| Question 4 OR 5 - Children's Language Development. A discursive essay on children's language development, with a choice of two questions where the data provided will focus on spoken, written or multimodal language. AO1: 15 marks, AO2: 15 marks. Total - 30 marks. | Question 4 - Write a/an ??? in which you assess the ideas and issues raised in Text A and Text B and argue your own views. (Opinion piece) AO2: 20 marks, AO5: 10 marks. Total - 30 marks. | |

Paper 1: Language, The Individual and Society

The first exam is all about how language is learned and how it is used as a tool for representation. It is worth 40% of your A-Level and has a total of 100 marks.

Theory: Language Levels

This section will give you all the information you need in order to apply language levels to a text you are analysing.

Lexis

Lexis is the study of words. Lexis means 'words' and so is the plural form; you may wish to describe a singular word, which is a 'lexeme'. Here is a table of all the key word classes you need to know:

Word class	Varieties	Definition	Example
Nouns - objects, people or things.	Common	General nouns (no capital letters needed).	cat, dog, book, exam.
	Proper	Nouns which need capital letters, like places and names.	Britain, Shakespeare.
	Concrete	Can be touched.	rock, pen, chair.
	Abstract	Cannot be touched.	love, hate, anger.
	Collective	Refers to a group.	flock, gaggle.
Verbs - actions.	Main	The main action of the sentence.	run, walk, swim.
	Verbal	Communicative actions.	speak, hear.
	Material	Events or actions.	write, watch.
	Dynamic	Actions which have definitive starts and ends.	run, watch.
	Mental and stative	Perceptions, cognitive processes and feelings.	think, feel, believe.

	Transitive	Have a direct object	I **went** for a run.
	Intransitive	Don't have a direct object.	I ran.
	Modal	Verbs which indicate a level of possibility or obligation.	may, can, must.
	Auxiliary	Verbs which assist the main verb.	be, do, have e.g. have eaten.
	Modal auxiliary	Verbs which both assist the main verb and indicate possibility and obligation.	may eat, could go.
	Copular	Linking verb.	be, is, was.
Adjectives - describing words.	Base	Simplest form.	high, cute, good.
	Comparative	Used to compare.	higher, cuter, better.
	Superlative	Used to indicate the most extreme form.	highest, cutest, best.
Adverbs - modifies a verb.	Time	Indicates **when** something occurs.	later, soon, yesterday.
	Place	Indicates **where** something occurs.	near, far, close.
	Manner	Indicates **how** something occurs.	boldly, lively, highly.
	Frequency	Indicates **how often** something occurs.	always, never, sometimes.
Conjunctions - joins clauses.	Coordinating	Joins two equal clauses.	for, and, nor, but, or, yet, so.
	Subordinating	Joins a subordinate clause.	although, however, whereas.
Prepositions	N/A	Indicates a position.	on, behind, below.
	Quantifiers	Gives a numerical value.	five, some, a few.

Determiners - modify a noun.	Demonstrative	Specify what is being referred to.	this, that, those.
	Definite	Something specific.	the – the dog.
	Indefinite	Something general.	a/an – a dog.

Pronouns:

	1st person		2nd person		3rd person	
	Subject	Object	Subject	Object	Subject	Object
Singular	I	me	you	you	he/she/it	him/her/it
Plural	we	us	you	you	they	them

Other forms:

	1st person		2nd person		3rd person	
	Singular	Plural	Singular	Plural	Singular	Plural
Possessive pronouns	mine	ours	yours		his/hers/its	Theirs
Possessive determiners	my	our	your		his/her/Its	Their
Reflexive pronouns	myself	ourselves	yourself		himself, herself, itself	Themselves

Relative pronouns:

These pronouns are used to introduce clauses which provide extra information (relative clauses) – who(m), which, that, whose.

All words are made up of morphemes, which are the smallest units of meaning. These come in the form of free/root morphemes, prefix-bound morphemes and suffix-bound morphemes. For example, the noun 'dogs' is made up as follows:

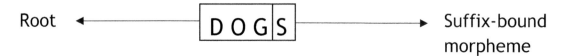

And in the adverb unfortunately:

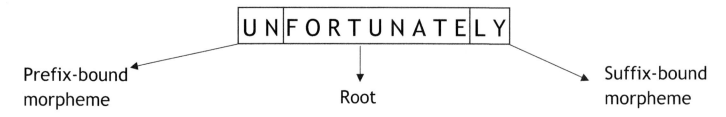

There is a special type of morpheme called an **inflection**. This is added to the end of an infinitive verb in order to change the tense as shown above. For example, 'walk' can become 'walk<u>ed</u>' or 'walk<u>ing</u>'.

Semantics

The topic of semantics is all about meaning. In its essence, it's about how lexis can be defined. Here are some key areas of semantics:

- **Semantic field** – a group of words/phrases with a common meaning.
- **Denotation** – dictionary definition.
- **Connotation** – the associated ideas with a word.
- **Synonym** – a word with the same meaning.
- **Antonym** – a word with the opposite meaning.
- **Collocation/collocates** – words which go together (salt and pepper)
- **Euphemism** – a less harsh way of saying things (for example, 'make love' instead of 'sex').
- **Dysphemism** – a blunt way of saying thing (for example, shag instead of sex).
- **Hypernym** – an umbrella/generic term (for example, animals).
- **Hyponym** – a part of a larger collection (for example, dogs).

Here is an example of a hypernym tree:

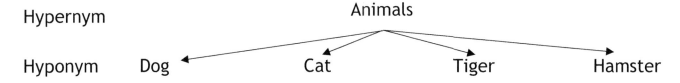

You could argue that the bottom row, as you could break those down further into breeds of dog, for example.

Pragmatics

Pragmatics is the study of what happens when you expand semantics and start considering ideas below what's on the surface. It is the study of the implied when the context is considered. For example, if I said 'It's 8pm', a semantic reading would argue that I was stating the time, however if I said this to a 7-year-old child, this could mean 'it's past your bedtime, you need to go to bed'.

When analysing a text, you should look to analyse what is being said which is implied and how that meaning is inferred. You should then think about how the context of an utterance alters the way in which it is read.

One area of pragmatics is the study of deixis – this is where the meaning of the word is completely dependent on the context. For example, in 'I went there yesterday', both 'there' and 'yesterday' are deictic as we would have to be in that conversation to fully understand what those words meant.

Another area is considering how people communicate with each other in accordance to rules. Grice stated that there was a **'cooperative principle'** in which there are four maxims (rules) which conversation must have to be successful. These are:

1. **The maxim of quality** – what is said must be truthful.
2. **The maxim of quantity** – what is said should be the right length – not too long or short.
3. **The maxim of relevance** – what is said should be relevant.
4. **The maxim of manner** – what is said should be clear (and not ambiguous).

Whilst many linguists dismiss Grice now (especially as many conversations do not abide to this – even using a metaphor flouts the maxim of quality!). Furthermore, linguists look at the way a person's 'face' is protected or threatened. By 'face', we mean a form of self-image, wants, desires and freedom. People can threaten our face in many ways. Positive face threatening acts attack when someone's self-image is damaged. For example, 'your essay isn't detailed enough' or 'your hair looks greasy'. Negative face threatening acts attack someone's freedom, wants and desires. For example, 'stop talking' and 'turn the TV off'.

Every speech act has the potential to be face-threatening, however, you could introduce a number of politeness strategies to reduce this. A speaker may use 'please' or indirect commands reduce how threatening an act is. For example, 'please could stop talking for a minute?' or 'I watched this episode last week'.

Grammar

Grammar is the study of how a language is structured when there is more than one word. Here is how language develops:

words → phrases → clauses → sentences → paragraphs → discourse

You can think of '→' as meaning 'makes up', if that aids your understanding.

Phrases are words which sit around a head word. So, for example, in the phrase, 'very angry ant', the key word is 'ant' - a noun, which, on its own, forms its own phrase - a **noun phrase**. However, within the noun phrase, there is an adjective, 'angry', which therefore forms an **adjective phrase** inside of the noun phrase – 'very angry'. Therefore, the noun phrase is made up of an adjective phrase and a noun.

There are many different types of phrases that you can have. These include **verb phrase**, **noun phrase**, **adjective phrase**, **adverb phrase** and **prepositional phrase**. Adjective phrases which come before the noun are called premodifiers, and those which come after the noun are called post-modifiers.

A clause is a collection of one or more phrases. Clauses can be one of three different types:

- **Main clause** (also called **independent clause**) – the core of the sentence – can exist on its own. For example, '**the dog wagged his tail**'.
- **Subordinate clause** (also called **dependant clause**) – exists as an addition to the main clause – it cannot exist without it. For example, '**barking and panting,** the dog wagged his tail'. You can usually spot them as they are introduced or ended with a comma.
- **Relative clause** – a clause which adds more information and is introduced by a relative pronoun. For example, 'the dog, **whose name is Milo,** wagged his tail'.
- **Parenthetical clause** – a clause which exists in brackets.

In addition, there are a number of different types of sentence:

- **Minor/fragment** – an incomplete sentence (missing one or more of SVO) – for example, 'sugar and milk?'.
- **Simple** – a main clause on its own. For example, 'the dog wagged his tail'.
- **Compound** – two or more simple sentences joined by a conjunction. For example, 'the dog wagged his tail and ran around the garden'.
- **Complex** – a sentence which contains at least one subordinate clause. For example, 'barking and panting, the dog wagged his tail and ran around the garden'.

When we write sentences in English, we modify how we write based on the time in which it took place – we do this without thinking. The tense you write in means our verbs look slightly different. Here are the different types of tenses you can use to identify when reading texts:

Tense	Type	Formation	Example
Past	Simple past	-ed	I played
	Past perfect	Had + ed	I had played
	Past progressive	Was + -ing	I was playing
	Past perfect progressive	Had been + -ing	I had been playing
Present	Simple present	Infinitive form	I play
	Present perfect	Have/has + -ed	I have played
	Present progressive	Am/is + -ing	I am playing
	Present perfect progressive	Have/has been + -ing	I have been playing
Future	Simple future	Will	I will play
	Future perfect	Will have + -ed	I will have played
	Future progressive	Will be + -ing	I will be playing
	Future perfect progressive	Will have been + -ing	I will have been playing

In English, all of our sentences follow an **SVO** order, which means there is always a subject, verb and object in that order. For example, 'Laura set the homework'.

In this sentence, 'Laura' is the subject, 'set' is the verb and 'the homework' is the object. In this, the subject, Laura is performing the action. This means it is written in the active voice. However, if we move the sentence around a bit, we get, 'the homework was set by Laura'.

In this sentence, Laura is still performing the action, but she is not in the subject position. Instead, she has moved to the object position and 'the homework' in now the subject; this is called the passive voice. Newspapers often use the passive voice to remove the actor. For example, it still makes sense to say 'the homework was set'.

You should look out for when a text uses passive voice and see if you can see where they are hiding some information. Writing about this will impress your examiner!

In addition, sentences can have different moods to display different functions. These are:
- **Interrogative** – used to ask a question – for example, 'What is your dog called?'
- **Declarative** – used to make statement – for example, 'My dog is called Milo.'
- **Imperative** – used to make a command – for example, 'Stop barking!'
- **Exclamative** – used to make an exclamation – for example, 'What a cute dog!'

However, the form of a sentence (what it looks like) may not match its function (what it does). For example, the sentence 'It's quite cold in here' may be a declarative, but it may be that the speaker wants the hearer to close the window, which would make it a disguised imperative.

Phonology

Phonology is the study of sounds – you will probably only encounter it during your study of Children's Language Development and region. The sounds which are produced are called phonemes. Here is a list of all the consonant phonemes:

IPA Symbol	Example
b	ball
d	day
ð (called thorn)	there
dʒ	jungle
f	fat
G	got
h	hop
j	yoghurt, student
K	cart
l	lunch
m	mow
n	note
ŋ	trying
p	pot
r	rubbish
s	song
ʃ	shut
t	teeth
tʃ	cheese
v	vase
w	walk
z	zebra
ʒ	pleasure, measure
θ (called theta)	think

Each phoneme in formed in a different way. There are two factors which influence how a consonant sound is produced - manner and place of articulation. Manner of articulation is the way in which a sound is produced, and the place of articulation is the place the sound is produced in the mouth. Here are the places of articulation:

- **Alveolar** – the tongue is placed just behind the teeth on the alveolar ridge.
- **Bilabial** – both lips are used.
- **Dental** – the tongue is on the teeth.
- **Glottal** – produced in the glottis (in the throat).
- **Labiodental** – combines the lips and teeth.
- **Palatal** – the tongue is on the roof of the mouth.
- **Post-alveolar** – the tongue is slightly further back from the alveolar ridge.
- **Velar** – the tongue is pressed against the back of the mouth.

Manner of articulation:

- **Fricative** – push of air.
- **Plosive** – quick start and stop of air.
- **Affricate** – starts as an affricate and ends as a plosive.
- **Nasal** – uses the nose.
- **Lateral** – air goes past the side of the tongue.
- **Approximant** – parts of the mouth are brought together but do not touch.

You can use this table in order to decipher where each sound is produced:

	Alveolar	Bilabial	Dental	Labiodental	Palatal	Post-Alveolar	Velar
Fricative	z s		ð θ	v f	dʒ	ʒ ʃ	
Plosive	d t	b p					g k
Affricate						tʃ	
Nasal	n	m					ŋ
Lateral	l						
Approximant	r	w			j		

The only sounds not included are /h/ and the glottal stop – both are produced in the glottal. All sounds which are in **bold** are sounds which are voiced – this means the vocal chords are needed to produce that sound.

Vowel sounds:

IPA symbol	Example
æ	Apple
aɪ	My
aʊ	House
ɑ:	Shard
ɒ	Knot
e	Met
eə	There
eɪ	Space
ə (called schwa)	Author, banana
əʊ	Owed
3:	Purse
i:	Bee
ɪ	Spit
ɪə	Clear
ɔ:	Chalk
ɔɪ	Toy
u:	Shoot
ʊ	Look
ʊə	Door
ʌ	Won

Unlike with consonants, you don't need to worry about learning how these are articulated!

Discourse structure

Discourse structure is the study of how a text is structured – how it goes from its start to its end. There are many different areas you can think about for this level. If you are thinking about the text as a whole, it may have the following structure:

- **Problem and solution** – the text poses a problem and then provides the solution
- **Cause and effect** – the text introduces an issue and the consequences of it
- **Cyclical** – the text ends on the same thread as it started
- **Narrative** – the text tells a story
- **Question and answer** – the text poses a question and then provides an answer.

If you are analysing a piece of speech, you may wish to consider various elements crucial to the structure of a speech, which may include:

- **Turn taking** – where speakers take turns to speak
- **Adjacency pairs** – pairs of conventional pieces of speech – the speaker will say one and the hearer will reply in a specific way. For example, speaker 1 may say 'hello' and speaker 2 would be expected to reply with another greeting.
- **Non-fluency features** – features which disrupt the flow of conversation. These may include:
  - **False starts** – the speaker starts to speak and then stops and retries that start. For example, 'John was eati- I saw John eating'.
  - **Repair** – the speaker makes a mistake and then corrects it. For example, 'Joe was writing – I mean reading'.
  - **Filler** – words which the speaker uses to gain time to think. For example, 'ummm', 'errr'.
  - **Back-channelling** – where a speaker passively agrees with what's being said. For example, 'yeah', 'uh-hum'.

In terms of internal text features, texts often use forms of referencing called anaphoric and cataphoric references. Anaphoric references look back at something in a text and cataphoric references look forward in a text. For example:

Alice walked to her desk. She stopped and stood in amazement.

Here, 'she' is an anaphoric reference, which refers back to Alice.

When she walked over to her desk, Alice stood there in amazement.

Here, 'she' is a cataphoric reference, which refers to the later use of Alice.

Graphology

Graphology is the study of how aesthetics are produced. This includes (but is not limited to):

- Font
- Size of text
- Images
- Colours
- Signs (the study of which is called semiotics)
- Space (both empty and filled!)

Graphology is often a very attractive area for you to explore - but it should not be a large part of your analysis. What's most important is your analysis of LANGUAGE.

Orthography

Orthography is the study of writing and the rules of writing. This includes:

- Spelling
- Capitalisation
- Letter formation
- Punctuation

Within a text, you can look at how a text uses or adapts norms. For example, a text may put certain lexis is all-capitals. This is called orthographic manipulation or manipulation of the orthographic norms.

Theory: Children's Language Development

Within the study of Children's Language Development, there are three key areas you need to know: learning to speak, learning to write and learning to read. This section will talk you through each section of the content.

Learning to speak

The first area of spoken acquisition you need to know is phonology. All the phonology content is covered for you in the earlier section of the book.

Before a child is even born, they are able to hear people talking. At approximately 16-18 weeks, the child can start hearing their mother and some of what people around her are saying. Once born, they acquire language in a number of stages:

1. **Instinctive biological noises** (0 to 6 weeks)
   a. These are noises which the baby does out of instinct rather than being in control.
   b. This is usually in the form of crying.

2. **Cooing and vocal play** (starts at approximately 7 weeks)
   a. The child starts to produce long vowel sounds, but these do not mean anything.
   b. The child starts putting sounds together (just playing) – this is called vocal play.

3. **Babbling** (begins at approximately 6 months)
   a. The child starts to **reduplicate** syllables – this is where the same sound is repeated. For example, 'baba', 'dada', 'mama'.
   b. Their caregiver usually starts praising them for this.
   c. The child starts to move on from that to mixing syllables. For example, 'damaba'. This is called variegated babbling.
   d. The child starts to produce lots of phonemes – this is called **phonemic expansion.**

      e. The child starts to use only the phonemes in their language – this is called **phonemic contraction**.

4. **Melodic utterances** (from 9 months onwards)
   a. The child starts to use **intonation**.
   b. The child starts to experiment with rhythm and tone.

5. **Protowords**
   a. The child starts to assign sounds to objects. These objects then become known as this. For example, 'pap' for the dog.

6. **The first word**
   a. The child finally produces their first fully formed word. Their parents get very excited and they produce that word over and over again.
   b. Common first words are dad, mum, cat, dog, teddy, baby and no.
   c. The holophrastic stage begins.

Children learn different phonemes at different rates. Sounds which are plosives and nasals are usually first to be acquired. As the child can see their parents' lips, they usually find bilabials easier to produce. This is usually followed by velar sounds and then fricative-related sounds. The last ones to be developed are usually theta (/θ/), thorn (/ð/) and /ʒ/.

After a child produces their first word, their journey to speech begins:

- **The Holophrastic Stage** – approximately 12 to 18 months
  - **Holophrases** are single words and usually nouns.
  - A single word can have many different meanings and moods. For example, a child shouting 'dog' could mean:
    - Where's the dog? (interrogative)
    - There's the dog. (declarative)
    - Come here, dog! (exclamative)

- o The child can add intonation, so if they say 'dog' and their voice rises at the end of the word, then you they might be asking a question.

- **The Two-Word Stage** – approximately 18 to 24 months
  - o As the title suggests, the child is now using 2 words.
  - o Verbs start to emerge more (and lots more nouns).
  - o The child begins to use syntax correctly, for example:
    - Subject and verb – Milo woof
    - Verb and object – bark dog
    - Noun phrases – soft Milo
    - Verb phrases – walk dog (but only verbs without inflections)

- **The Telegraphic Stage** – approximately 24 months until 5 years
  - o This is when there are just enough words to successfully communicate – think telegram.
  - o There is a massive increase in vocabulary in the section.
  - o Many word classes now acquired like pronouns, prepositions and various determiners but often omitted. For example:
    - Milo is dog
    - Milo go(es) woof
    - Where dog go?
  - o As a child comes to the end of this stage, they start to become more complex with their language, adding negatives, inflections and coordinating conjunctions.

- The Post-Telegraphic Stage/Complex-Utterance Stage
  - o At this stage, the child can use many advanced features of English, including contractions and irregular verbs.

When learning to speak, children often make mistakes. Sometimes these mistakes are to make the word easier to pronounce. These mistakes fall into 5 different categories:

1. **Addition** – the child adds something completely new into the pronunciation. For example, 'cat-o' (cat + o).
   a. There is a process of addition called **diminutisation** where a child adds a 'y' onto the end of words to make them **diminutives**. For example, 'doggy'.

2. **Deletion** – the child removes a sound from the word altogether. For example, 'ca' (instead of cat).

3. **Consonant cluster reduction** – the child removes some consonant sounds from the word. For example, 'ra-it' instead of 'rabbit'.

4. **Substitution** – the child substitutes an easier phoneme in place of a easier one. For example, 'loghurt' instead of yoghurt.

5. **Assimilation** – the child uses a sound from earlier or later in the word as it is easier to say. For example, 'lellow' instead of yellow.

However, it is important to note that children often do not know they are simplifying. The fis-fish phenomenon which you can find in the table below.

Once a child has acquired language, it is important to look at what they use it for. Halliday describes 7 core functions that children use language for in the order they acquire it:

1. **Instrumental** – the child needs something – for example, 'want drink' and 'need toilet'.
2. **Regulatory** – the child wants something to happen – for example, 'pass me juice', 'come here'.
3. **Interactional** – the child interacts with others – for example, 'doggy play?', 'love you mummy'.
4. **Personal** – the child wants to express themselves – for example, 'doggy good boy', 'me no like cheese'.
5. **Heuristic** – the child wants to learn about the world – for example, 'what dog doing?', 'where dad going?'.
6. **Imaginative** – the child wants to be creative with language, including telling stories – for example, 'me a doggy too! Woof woof!', 'one day when I was...'.
7. **Representational** - the child wants to relay facts – for example, 'I am 2', 'dog is on sofa'

General speech acquisition theories:

Name	Ideas, concept and theories
Mehler	Babies recognised their parents' language when they were born.
O'Grady	Children struggle to distinguish between /r/ and /w/ up to the age of 7.
Berko and Brown	Children notice when caregivers make mistakes but are unable to see that they are making a mistake. A child was saying 'fis' and when asked if they meant 'fis', they said no, but when asked if they meant 'fish', they said yes.
Rescorla	There are 3 different types of overextension: 1. **Categorical** – the child applies a label to everything in a category. For example, 'dog' for all animals 2. **Analogical** – the child applies a label to everything which is physically or visually similar. For example, 'tomato' for a ball. 3. **Relational** – the child applies a label which is in some form related to the object. For example, 'pen' for paper.
Belugi	The child fronts negatives, for example, 'no me go outside' when first learning to negate.
Lenneberg	There is a critical period for learning language – after this point, it very difficult to learn.

Cruttenden	Learning to use inflections correctly comes in the form of a u-shaped curve:
	At 1: the child uses an inflection and gets it right At 2: the child applies it everywhere and gets it wrong At 3: the child learns when to use it correctly

There is a HUGE debate in spoken acquisition as to how a child learns language. This section will take you through the 5 main schools of thought.

Behaviourism

What do they argue?
Children learn through positive and negative reinforcement. When a child says something right, their caregivers will praise them and when they say something wrong, they will tell them it's wrong and correct them.

Who is the main theorist?
Skinner

How can I spot this in data?
Look for where the caregiver positively or negatively reinforces language.

Interactionalism

What do they argue?
Children are born with nothing (tabula rasa) and learn language from the social environment they are in – this includes caregivers providing support.

Who is the main theorist?
Bruner – he developed the Language Acquisition Support System (LASS) – which is designed for caregivers to scaffold and support a child's language to help them get it correct. When using language to talk to a child, we call this Child Directed Speech (CDS). This includes:

- Labelling - providing the label, for example, 'that's a ball'.
- Over-articulation - elongating vowel sounds, for example, 'baby's foooooooood'.
- Echoing – repeating what the child says.
- Expansion – repeating what the child said, but in a more linguistically sophisticated way, for example, 'doggy chew' → 'yes, that's right, the dog is chewing'.
- Expatiation – repeating what the child said but adding more information, for example, 'bottle cold' → 'yes, the bottle is cold, so I'll warm it up for you'.
- Reformulation – repeating what the child says, but in a different way, for example, 'doggy tail wag' → 'is the dog wagging his tail?'.

What concepts, ideas and theories support and challenge it?

Name	Concept, idea and theory
Snow	Coined the term 'motherese' to describe the way mothers talk to their children. This includes: • Higher pitch • Greater range of **intonation** • Frequent use of the **interrogative and declarative mood** • Repetition of syllables and phrases

Bard and Sachs	Case study of Jim – a boy with two deaf parents. They exposed him to TV and radio to hear language, but he didn't learn how to speak. However, interactions with speech therapists allowed him to acquire language, thus proving the importance of interaction.
Snarey	Fathers play with their children in more physical and less linguistic ways.
Myszor	CDS helps **social development**, but not linguistic development.
Trevarthen	Children learn turn taking before they learn language as a result of CDS.
Chomsky	Children produce utterances which abide to no grammatical structure. No caregiver would have said their utterance, so there must be something external to caregivers.

How can I spot this in data?

Look for:

- Caregivers correcting children and children either adopting or rejecting the change.
- Caregivers using elements of motherese, LASS or CDS.

Nativism

What do they argue?
There is some form of in-built language learning device.

Who is the main theorist?
Chomsky – he argues that children do not learn through imitation and that even if they did, caregivers do not provide a good enough source of English – he calls this a **poverty of stimulus**. He argues that children have a **Language Acquisition Device (LAD)** in their brains which helps them to acquire language and contains a set of rules about how to use grammar and that as children become more exposed to language, different parts of their LAD activate. He calls this **Universal Grammar**. He furthers his theory by saying that children say things with mistakes that an adult would never have said, which means they cannot be imitating. For example, 'I threwed the ball'. He calls these virtuous errors – errors where you can see why they have this wrong.

What concepts, ideas and theories support it?

Name	Concept, idea and theory
Pinker	When a child produces an utterance, almost every single utterance is new – they cannot be imitating.
Pye	Cultures around the world raise children differently – including some which don't use CDS – yet they all learn to speak. This suggests there is something innate at play.
Berko-Gleason	**The Wug Test** Children were shown pictures of a fictional things and actions and asked to form the object or action using an inflected ending. For example: There is one WUG. There are two _____. The majority (75%) of child aged 4-5 were able to choose the right ending. This means therefore, that children do not learn through imitation

Case study: Genie	Genie was a child who was abused until the age of 13 – shut away and deprived of human contact. Linguists worked with her, but since she had passed the critical period, she couldn't learn language. This suggests that there must be some form of internal structure as caregivers were unable to help Genie to acquire language.

HOWEVER, there is no scientific proof that this exists. Chomsky based his theory on his observations only.

How can I spot this in data?
Look for:

- Children resisting being corrected OR children which accept correction and then revert back again.
- Mistakes with inflections.
- Children making virtuous errors.

Cognitivism

What do they argue?
Children need to be cognitively adept to talk about things; they cannot express what they do not understand.

Who is the main theorist?
Piaget – he argues that until children learn the rule of object permanence (things still exist when you can't see them), they struggle to name things; hence why children's language starts to be acquired properly at around a year.

What concepts, ideas and theories support it?

Name	Concept, idea and theory
Vygotsky	Children have a cognitive deficiency – they need to understand things and have a gap of knowledge. He calls this the **Zone of Proximal Development (ZPD)**. He argues that the role of the caregiver (or, as he describes, a **More Knowledgeable Other (MKO)** is to fill the cognitive gap.

However, children who have learning difficulties still manage to acquire one.

How can I spot this in data?
Look for:

- Children who are struggling to say something they are unlikely to understand.
- Caregivers explaining something to children.

Social constructivism

What do they argue?
Children learn the rules of language and learn to construct it.

Who is the main theorist?
Tomasello – children listen to language and find patterns and develop plans on how language is used (schemas).

Braine – children learn to use slots and frames. As Tomasello says, these schemas are developed from listening to adults. These could look like this:

When I want to talk about myself having completed an action:
'I + (SLOT)ed'

Where a verb can be added into the slot to form utterances like:
'I liked', 'I played', 'I jumped', 'I threwed'.

How can I spot this in data?
Look for:

- Children making virtuous errors
- Formulaic expressions

Learning to read

Key terminology:

- **Grapheme-Phoneme Correspondence** – where the sounds match with the letters, for example, 'dog' has grapheme-phoneme correspondence, but 'gnome' does not.
- **Phonic approach** – used to help children read aloud – children are encouraged to spell out the word by recognising what **graphemes** (letters), **digraphs** (two letters) and **trigraphs** (three letters) correspond to what phonemes
- **Whole-word approach** – used to help children to read – they are encouraged to look and say. It relies on children memorising large numbers of words
- **Psycholinguistic approach** – used to help children to read – they are encouraged to decode words based on their context (other words, pictures, etc).

Theories on reading:

Name	Idea, concept and theory
Gough	Readers convert graphemes to phonemes and produce meaning that way.
Goodman	Readers make hypotheses about what may happen which can be accepted or rejected.
LaBerge and Samuels	Readers store letters, consonant clusters and words which are linked to phonemic equivalents and their semantic meaning in their memory.
Klein et al	Before reading, readers will try to guess purpose, form and genre.
Clay	Children will spot where they have made a mistake when reading aloud – this will trigger them to go back and correct it.
Ehri	There are four stages to learning to reading:

	1. **Pre-alphabetic** – only some letters are recognised. 2. **Partial-alphabetic** – more letters are recognised and phonemes are starting to be attached. 3. **Full-alphabetic** – all letters recognised and new words can be decoded. 4. **Consolidated-alphabetic** – almost all new words can be decoded, especially longer ones.
Marsh, Friedman, Welch, and Desberg	There are four stages to learning to read: **Stage 1** – Words are learned – the child has no sense of phoneme-grapheme correspondence. **Stage 2** – Graphemes begin to influence how the child reads the word. **Stage 3** – Letters are decoded to sounds. **Stage 4** – The child uses stage 3 and context to decipher the word.
Frith	There are three stages to learning to read: 1. **Logographic** – words are recognised as objects 2. **Alphabetic** – the idea of letters develops. Child starts to associate graphemes with phonemes. 3. **Orthographic** – the child can recognise words and patterns with phoneme-grapheme correspondence.
Stuart	Argues that Frith's logographic stage doesn't exist.
Chall	There are six stages to learning to read: 0. **Pseudo reading** – the child retells stories it has been read. (Before six years) 1. **Decoding** – understands that words have phoneme-grapheme correspondence. Sounds words out. (6-7 years) 2. **Fluency** – simple texts can be read, greater amount of words learned by sight. (7-8 years)

	3. **Learning** – the child uses reading to learn. (8-14 years)
	4. **Multiple viewpoints** – can read texts with different viewpoints. (14-18 years)
	5. **Construction and reconstruction** – can be critical and analytical of texts. (Older than 18)

Learning to write

Key terminology:

- **Insertion** – a (spurious) letter is added which does not belong in the word.
- **Omission** – a letter is missed from the word which should be there.
- **Substitution** – a letter is substituted in for another letter.
- **Graphemic cluster omission** – a cluster of letters has been omitted from the word.
- **Graphemic cluster substitution** – a cluster of letters has been substituted for another set.
- **Transposed letters** – a letter has been written the wrong way round.
- **Cursive** – joining up letters when writing.
- **Magic e** – the <e> at the end of words which is silent, for example, 'make', 'cake'.
- **Hypotaxis** – joining clauses using subordination.
- **Parataxis** – simple sentences joined with no conjunctions or coordinating conjunctions.

Here are the key theories in writing:

Name	Idea, concept and theory
Kroll	There are four stages to writing acquisition: - **The Preparatory Stage** – 18 months to 6 years. The child acquires basic motor skills (like holding a pen) and the basic rules of spelling. - **The Consolidation Stage** – 6 years to 8 years. Writing is speech-like. Sentences are usually short and declaratives. Punctuation doesn't exist. Writing is paratactical. - **The Differentiation Stage** – 8 years to 16 years. The child can differentiate between spoken and written modes. Control and mastery of spelling, punctuation and grammar grows as this stage continues.

	• **The Integration Stage** – 16 years +. The child can write with almost complete accuracy of spelling, punctuation and grammar. Their writing is individual and personal.
Barclay	There are 7 stages to writing development: 1. **Scribbling** – random squiggles on the page – not related to letters in any way. 2. **Mock handwriting** – the squiggles are now in the form of shapes. 3. **Mock letters** – the child produces pseudo letters – these look like letters. 4. **Conventional letters** – the child produces proper letters and begins to learn grapheme-phoneme correspondence. Sometimes the first letter of a word is written to represent the entire word. 5. **Invented spelling** – the child spells how words sound – this is sometimes correct, but often wrong. 6. **Appropriate spelling** – writing is now often including complex sentences and spelling is often quite accurate. 7. **Correct spelling** – most spelling is correct.
Clay	There are a number of concepts a child needs to grasp: • **Sign concept** – writing carries meaning. • **Message concept** – what is spoken can be written. • **Space concept** – words need spaces between them. • **Direction concept** – writing is done from left to right.
Rothery	There are four categories a child may use to write in: 1. **Narratives** – a story which follows a structure. 2. **Reports** – factual accounts. 3. **Recounts** – chronological accounts. 4. **Observations** – comments on what they have seen.

Treiman	The child's own name is important to it – they will often add a capital letter in sentences where the first letter of their name appears.
National curriculum	The government provide schools and teachers with expected standards of how a child should write – this is focused on accuracy, rather than creativity. This holds the view that accuracy is something which can be measured.
Maley	Believes that creative writing is a crucial part of learning to write as it allows children to play with language.
Abbot	Compares not allowing children to be creative to battery hens – they have no freedom and so won't produce as good a quality as those with freedom.
Britton	Children need creative freedom in order to learn to write.
Bryce-Heath	Compared how caregivers viewed literacy development in three different towns: • **Trackton** – black working class. There was a big culture of creative oral narratives rather than reading. This resulted in the children becoming excellent story makers but struggled with writing. • **Roadville** – white-working class. The parents provided educational books for their children. The children started off well but struggled as time went on. • **Maintown** – white-middle class. The parents provided lots of different types of books and encouraged literacy development. Their children excelled in school.
Crystal	Compares writing to feeling like they are in a jailhouse, but creative writing is the key.
Goouch and Lambirth	A child's self-esteem will suffer if they are told their writing is 'wrong'.
Rickford	Rules are important and necessary in learning to write.
Torrance	Assessment leads to better writing, so accuracy is important.

Exam walkthrough

Section A

Section A is worth 70 marks and is split 25-25-20 between the first three questions.

This is a textual analysis question and you will receive **two texts**; one contemporary and one historical. The earliest a text could come from is 1600. The text may be spoken, written or multimodal (a discussion board, for example).

The first to note is a big one – quotations. The examiner **WILL NOT** reward you for comments like 'the text uses high-frequency monosyllabic lexis to...' because there is no evidence. You **MUST** provide a quotation for everything you label. Also, remember that 'quote' is a verb and 'quotation' is a noun. You have a quotation, not a quote! You should also remember to only use quotations which fully support your point. You should be selective in the quotations you use – choose the ones which are going to best support your point!

You should avoid using lengthy quotations – if you're proving a type of sentence, go for the first two words, an ellipsis and the last two words, so the examiner knows where you're quoting from. For example, "If you thought ... no way!". You should also avoid repeating expressions like 'a quotation to show this is'. Vary the way you start your sentences – here are a few you can use:

- 'This is exemplified in...'
- 'An example being...'
- 'For example, ...'
- 'As is seen in...'

Avoid writing an introduction for any of these questions. Introductions for these questions are rarely useful and distract you from what you're being asked to do! By all means, state the genre, register, audience, subject, purpose, mode and era, but use them **in your analysis,** as a link to context. I would recommend writing them down at the top of your answer booklet and ticking them off when you've mentioned them. Thinking logically, if you're just stating that it's an article, you're not answering anything. Launch straight into your analysis – this will help you to get the marks.

When writing about something like mode, be very careful that it is relevant to the point you are making. Remember you're telling the examiner as many **relevant** pieces of information as possible. It's not going to get you an A* by stating that an article is using the written mode, because this is obvious. If you do want to look at mode, you could look at how language which we would expect in the spoken mode seeps into the written mode and vice versa.

You should also be very careful in making generalisations. Whilst it is perfectly fine to state that a publication has political bias, it is not okay to state things like 'readers of the Daily Mail are right wing'. This simply isn't true. Likewise, making sweeping generalisations about history are not suitable either: statements like 'women in the 19th century were obsessed with hair' is both factually inaccurate, unsupported and counter-productive. Instead, look at how the text is addressing stereotypes and how this is being represented.

In addition, do not organise your analysis with language levels. This prevents you from answering the question. It's fantastic that you can tell the examiner all about the wonderful lexical features of the text, but if you're not linking this to meanings or representations, then you are not answering the question! Stick to the structure which is below as this will help you to fully answer the question and pick up the marks.

Avoid spending large amounts of time writing about the relevance of adherence to Late Modern English (for example) orthographic conventions unless it is **RELEVANT** to the point you're making. It's fantastic that you can label a medial 's', but if it's not linked to the point which you're making, you're wasting your time.

Finally, read the texts **CAREFULLY**. It is very important that you understand what they are trying to tell you. Remember that whilst you're answering for an English Language exam, this question does not require theory, so leave it out, even if you can name an associated theory. This is especially true on texts which play into things you may have studied in gender. This is purely a textual analysis question.

Question 1 and 2

WHAT DOES IT LOOK LIKE?
Analyse how Text A uses language to create meanings and representations.

WHAT IS ASSESSED?
These questions are worth **25 marks**. 10 marks are for **AO1** and 15 marks are for **AO3**.

The important difference between the two questions is that Text B will be a historical text.

For each text, you should find 3-4 things that are being REPRESENTED. These could be:

- The subject of the text
- The text producer
- A person, event or place
- A culture
- The publisher (for example, the newspaper)

Once you have these written down, you need to ask yourself one KEY question:

What specific uses of language has the author used to represent this?

And now is when you can get out your lexical and syntactic analysis skills. Pick out specific examples of where language is being used to represent something and think about a contextual point which you can make to support you on this.

Your success on this question will be determined by your ability to link language with context.

Once you have done that, now you can begin to write your answer. Here is how I recommend starting each point:

> Within the text, (thing being represented) is represented as (adjective). This is being done through the use of (language feature), for example "QUOTE". This is significant because... (link to context).

Your links to context may include, but is not limited to:

- Genre
- Audience
- Purpose
- Subject
- Social context
- Cultural context
- Journalistic context
- Time (question 2, only)

Here are two examples of the starts of paragraphs:

> Within the text, Donald Trump is represented as irresponsible. This is being done through the use of the adjectives like 'idiotic' which can be linked to the context because the purpose of the article is to report on his actions, which the newspaper would like to represent in a negative way. This can also be see with the use of...
>
> The Telegraph is representing and positioning themselves as a reliable source of knowledge in their use of the elliptical clause 'Always link ... the context...' which has links to the social and cultural context as at the time in which the article was produced, there was an upsurge the awareness of 'fake news' and therefore, it is important for The Telegraph to be seen to be producing accurate and truthful news and the use of this elliptical clause demonstrates this to their readers.

Question 3

WHAT DOES IT LOOK LIKE?
Explore the similarities and differences in the ways that Text A and Text B use language.

WHAT IS ASSESSED?
This question is worth **20** marks and all 20 marks are for **AO4**.

Question 3 is one of the most difficult questions on the exam. The important thing to note is that although you're being assessed on AO4, it is informed by AO1 and AO3, so you still need examples from the text. You can, however, still use examples that you have used in the previous questions.

In order to plot out what to say, answer the following questions:

- How is the language used different in the texts?
- How is the context different? How does the time difference impact on the use of language?
- How can we see a change in attitudes between the two texts? How is this reflected in the language?

The question is asking for comparison, so don't forget to compare, but simply comparing language isn't enough – you need to compare language with context together.

For this question, you do not need to carry out lots of language labelling if this is not relevant to the question. Much as in the previous question, you need to link language to context when you are comparing. If you always keep language and context together when you are comparing, you will do well on this question.

Section B

This section is worth 30 marks and assesses at Children's Language Development.

Question 4 and 5

WHAT DOES IT LOOK LIKE?

'statement on language'.

Referring to the data in detail, and to relevant ideas from language study, evaluate this view of children's language development.

WHAT IS ASSESSED?

These questions are worth **30** marks each and you should answer **ONLY ONE** of them. 15 marks are for **AO1** and 15 marks are for **AO2**.

In the exam, you will be presented with two questions with data. The data will be spoken, written or multimodal. At the time of writing, the data has always been one question on learning to speak and another question on learning to write, however, there are no assurances from the exam board that this format will stay the same.

If you have not been taught anything other than spoken, **DO NOT** answer any other question. You will struggle to answer the question and you will get a poor mark as a result.

You should approach the answering this question in the following order:

1. Read the question and the statement
2. Read the data
3. Find areas where the data agrees with the statement
4. Find areas where the data disagrees with the statement
5. Link elements of the data to the theory you have studied.

Then, and this is the important part...

PLAN YOUR ANSWER!

It is **VITAL** that you do this. Plot where you are going to bring in each school of thought and what evidence you will provide. As you're planning, ask yourself:

Am I directly answering the question with this point?

If not, rethink it. Make sure that everything falls in line with the question and what you're arguing.

As with all analysis questions in English Language, make sure you incorporate the data into your line of argument. Explain how the data links with the theory.

Make sure that when you're picking out a phoneme, label it as much as you can and that you make a link. Don't forget that some phonemes have special names (schwa, theta, thorn etc) and it's always good to use these!

If you can't remember a theorist's name, still write the theory – the examiner may still reward you.

Revise the **ages** and **stages** – these can help you contextualise the child(ren). Remember that whilst it's often good to use these, writing things like 'as the child is 3;6, they are in the Post-telegraphic stage' may not be true, you may find that they are actually only in the telegraphic stage. Always use evidence. Where possible integrate their stage into one of your points – try not to just randomly state it. For example:

Although Daniel is 3;6 and should, according to Crystal, be in the post-telegraphic stage, he displays some features of language which imply that he may still be telegraphic stage. For example... This may be seen as evidence of the way in which caregiver interactions are hindering Daniel's development.

In order for you to get the top grades, you need to evaluate the view and the theories you are writing about. A great place to do this is in the conclusion, but you don't have to wait until the conclusion to start evaluating – you can do it as you go. You could write about why Chomsky's research is flawed. You could use the data to refute Bruner. The best candidates see the complexity of the issues wherever they can.

If you aren't sure what to write in your introduction, leave it until last. Your introduction should introduce the ideas which you'll be discussing in your essay as well as what your argument will be. If the statement references a specific theory, make sure you include that theory in the introduction.

When writing a conclusion, actually conclude. It's pointless for you to repeat what you've said in your essay and is not what constitutes a conclusion. In a conclusion, you should weigh up and evaluate the statement. How far do you agree? What does the data say? What do the theorists say?

To structure your essay, please see page 94 on 'prove, support, refute, evaluate'.

Exam timings

You should spend **20 minutes** reading the texts through first.
Then you should spend **30 minutes** on each of **question 1 and 2**.
You should then spend **20 minutes** on **question 3**.

You should spend **10 minutes** reading and annotating data for **question 4/5**.
You then have **40 minutes** to answer the question. This should be divided as follows:

- **5 minutes planning**
- **35 minutes writing**

ANY TIME LEFT SPARE SHOULD BE USED TO CHECK YOUR ANSWERS

You may find it quite useful to write the timings on your exam paper at the start. For example, if the exam starts at 9AM, you would write:

9 - text A
9:10 – Q1
9:40 – text B
9:50 – Q2
10:20 – Q3
10:40 - data
10:50 – Q4/5

Doing this means you have very clear goalposts and you won't spend too long on any question.

Practice exam questions

Debate prompts for **spoken acquisition**:

- 'A child cannot learn through imitation'.
- 'Child directed speech hinders more than it helps'.
- 'Correcting a child does not help them'.
- 'Caregiver interactions have a negative impact on a child'.
- 'A child needs to get something wrong in order to get it right'.
- 'Caregivers provide a poor input for children to learn language'.
- 'There is an external force from caregivers which helps a child to learn to speak'.
- 'Syntactic development is more important than phonological development'.

Debate prompts for **written acquisition and learning to read**:

- 'The role of caregivers is instrumental in a child learning to read and write'.
- 'It is more important to be creative than it is to be accurate'.
- 'Accuracy should predate creativity'.
- 'Understanding grammar is a vital part of learning to write'.
- 'Letter formation is crucial in learning to write'.
- 'Learning to read is an important part in learning to speak'.
- 'A child needs to be corrected when learning to write'.

Model essay plans

These are just examples of plans, in the exam these would be in note form. I have imagined there is data to support these plans.

Question prompt: A child cannot learn through imitation.

Prove:
- Define imitation.
- Contextualise data.
- Briefly mention Bruner and LASS.
- Briefly mention Chomsky – set up debate.

Support:
- Chomsky – LAD. Use data to show that the child does its own thing and resists correction.
- Chomsky – Poverty of stimulus. Use data to show that child produces utterances which could not be imitations.
- Pye – some cultures don't engage in imitation and their children still learn to speak fine.

Refute:
- Bruner – LASS + Snow. Explain that caregivers often get the child to imitate them. Use data to show how caregiver interaction is a system of support and imitation.
- Piaget – child would struggle to articulate and imitate if they do not understand. Vygotsky – imitation could help fill ZPD.

Evaluate:
- Mostly disagree with the statement. Imitation helps understanding, even if the role is little.
- Link Tomosello and Braine – the child imitates the sentence frames only.

Question prompt: A child needs to be corrected when learning to write

Prove:
- Mention the role of caregivers in helping a child – mention school environment.
- Mention the importance of accuracy
- Contextualise data.

Support:
- National curriculum – measures accuracy.
- Torrance – assessment = better writing. Link data.
- Rickford – importance of rules. Link data.

Refute:
- Goouch and Lambirth – esteem. Link Crystal's jailhouse metaphor. Link data.
- Britton – need for freedom. Link Abbot.

Evaluate:
- Agree to an extent – accurate writing is important in the long run, but...
- This shouldn't be at the expense of creativity.

Model essays

Text A is taken from the 'Daily Express', a publication which is famously right-wing. As a result of this social and political context, values represent their publication, and there is a certain expectation for readers of what these values are and stand for. In the text, they talk about the decline in values, something which right-wing publications like to talk about. The Daily Express is represented as the voice of the people through the use of the first person inclusive plural pronoun "we" which is repeated as a pattern throughout the text. This pattern is designed to represent the Daily Express as being on the level as the reader. In addition, they use the anecdote of being on "the busy train to work" in order to appeal to their readers by giving them something they can relate to. This is especially true of considering the Daily Express is popular in London – a place which many readers will commute to work on the said "busy trains". Also, the text uses parallel clauses in "in we're not...collect the kids", with the repetition of the phrases "if we're not" and "then we're" in two finite clauses. In doing this, they are strengthening their argument to the reader, and tapping into more relatable situations for the reader. This is evidence of aspects of context working together to influence the language used – if it wasn't relevant to the reader, their point would be less effective.

In addition, the text creates an 'us and them' structure to group the audience and the text producer into a single group against the so-called "louts". They do this by creating a contrast between pronouns, for example, in the declarative sentence "if people ... into them", each subordinate clause ends with a different pronoun. The first ends with the first person plural pronoun "us" and then ends with third person plural pronoun "them". This is all helped by the fact that the author of the piece, Jo Byrant, has her name post-modified with "etiquette ... manners", designed to elevate the status of her and position her as knowledgeable to the reader. The alliterative "Modern Manners" draws particular attention to the subordinate clause which emphasises Byrant's expertise by include "A-Z" to imply complete coverage.

The text's main concern is with decline of politeness, and this can be seen as well as on the surface at a semantical level, in the pragmatic functions. The text is consumed by the use of anaphoric references like in adverbs of time like "once" and in the past tense verb of "were" which look back to a time in which the Daily Express believe society was more polite. In addition, they use two pictures which are graphologically contrasting. One of David Cameron who, whilst not being prime minister at the time, was known to the public, especially those right-wing readers of the Daily Express, as he had a prominent role in the Conservative party. The photo has him being treated poorly by who the Daily Express (indirectly) blame for the decline in politeness. This is then contrasted with children who are obedient. What's particularly interesting is the use of orthographic manipulation in "POLITE" which is drawing particular emphasis to the abstract noun and is what the Daily Express desire.

Examiner comments:

AO1: Recognises patterns in grammar. 10 marks.

AO3: Evaluates attitudes of writer, linked to wider social attitudes and values of the Express. 15 marks.

Total score: 25/25.

June 2018, question 2. Data and question available on the AQA website.

In Text B, Green responds to the publication of an article about "rudeness of women to women". In this, she anecdotally describes a journey on a bus and her encounter with a conductress. Green represents the conductress as incorrect and rude through the construction of dialogue. Towards the end of the text, Green presents dialogue from both and "old lady" and the conductress, which allows the reader to examine the speech in parallel. In particular, the use of the adjective "old" connotes vulnerability, and this increases the power of Green's argument against the conductress.

 The dialogue of the conductress is written phonologically with the conversion of the standard lexis to a harder-to-read lexis, for example, the change from the second person possessive pronoun "your" to the phonetic "yer" in the text, and the contracted "there's" rather than the standard 'there is'. This represents the conductress as unintelligible, especially in contrast to the very formal writing in the piece, which adheres to standard formal English. At the time in which this is written, World War One had created a large amount of social upheaval and created a sense of social mobility. As a result, there was a greater mix of classes mixing with each other, and as a result, we see the more affluent upper class protesting about the lower class. This is especially true when you examine the fact that Green's entire argument rests on this encounter with the conductress. In this case, her grievance with the conductress and rudeness is a proxy argument for the increase in social mobility.

The text reinforces representations of the conductress by the representations of the other women she mentions, including herself. Green premodifies the work these women do with the base adjective "splendid", in order to accentuate the work of the women against the work of the conductress. In the language she uses, Green presents herself as quite affluent. Her strings of complex sentences in the declarative mood (e.g. "they wood hard... their spirit") at the start of the text form a pattern and state her opinion as fact. This then turns to a complexity as the text progresses and at the end, we see the declarative mood return, but with the simple sentence "men have ... other" and the minor sentence "they are right". This final minor sentence ends the piece strongly and allows the reader to reflect on the behaviour of women, particularly in respect to their metaphorical representation as cats. In addition, Green uses the polysyllabic, low frequency, high register lexis like "remonstrated" which is virtually non-existent in the current context, and was likely not overly present at the time Green writes. This positions Green as knowledgeable and therefore her opinion as valid and well-constructed.

Examiner comments:

AO1: Identifies patterns and integrates different levels, as student doesn't address grammar in detail, but credited with a more integrated response. 9 marks.

AO3: Evaluates wider social contexts, including attitudes to class. See complexities as part of a bigger social picture. 15 marks.

Total mark: 24/25

June 2018, question 3. Data and question available on the AQA website.

Both texts present attitudes towards politeness, and despite their time difference of 90 years, there are several parallels within the texts. Both texts are concerned with the upholding of politeness. Culturally, British people are known for being extremely polite, and many people view this as a core British value. Therefore, the representation of the issue towards people in both texts reflect the lack of change in attitudes towards politeness. The verb phrase "make life intolerable" in text A and the verb phrase in text B "have to contend" both show this. If anything, the issue is slightly exaggerated in text A, with the adjective "intolerable" intensifying the pain which Bryant feels. In contrast, in text B, the letter (originally) form in which it was written doesn't suit the sensationalised style of the newspaper article in text A.

However, the place at which we place the blame is different. The changing nature of who we blame for poor politeness is shown through the representation of the ones who are rude. In text B, the title immediately states where the issue is coming from - women. Throughout the piece, women are the ones who are the ones referred to as the problem, with the only mention of a man being at the end and his comment on the behaviour of women. Whereas in text A, the blame is placed with young people. Text A has to be more mindful of its blame though, as the article can be shared on Facebook and Twitter which are used by the young people they are blaming. Text B does not have this issue as it is printed in the newspaper.

Examiner comments:

AO4: Sees big picture of discourses about rudeness - similarities and differences. Direct comparison of language at times and a sense that language analysis supports the contextual connections. Brief response, prevents consistent evaluation.

Total mark: 14/20.

June 2017, question 4. Data and question available on the AQA website.

The debate over whether nature or nurture dominates a child's language development continues to divide linguists. Child directed speech is an element of the nurture debate, as part of the interactionalist approach popularised by linguists like Snow and Bruner. They face challenge from nativists like Chomsky who believe that an inborn faculty dominates development of language. The data set can illuminate this debate, with the 1'2 Jayce's interactions with his mother offering an insight into the use of CDS.

At this stage in his development, Jayce should know around 50 to 100 words (Crystal), with him just leaving the holophrastic stage (Crystal). However, reduplication dominates Jayce's side of the conversation, thus we are left with largely the speech the mother. Snow coined the term 'motherese' to describe the language of mothers when communicating to their children. Mother in the transcript exhibits a number of motherese features, for example, the "sing song voice" which causes the change in intonation, something which causes brain activity to peak. In addition, the mother repeatedly uses the question formation structure. Snow would argue that, this is teaching Jayce the 'question and 'answer' structure of conversation. Additionally, Braine would argue that it is teaching Jayce a 'slot and frame' schema for questions through the use of "where's the balloon?" and "where's the banana?". These theorists would argue that because children are born 'tabula rasa', it is this child directed speech which causes development.

Quite interestingly, when Jayce says "nana", he uses deletion of the alveolar plosive /bə/ from the start of the phrase. His mother then recasts it for him, as Bruner would argue is part of LASS. She then says that Jayce can't form the /bə/ phoneme, despite saying it earlier to represent "ball". Vygotsky would describe this as a zone of proximal development, as Jayce needs the MKO to fill the gap of knowledge that 'ball' and 'banana' reuse the same phoneme. However, if what Snow and her nurture linguists say is correct, then why does Jayce barely respond? Throughout the transcript, Jayce's responses are minimal and are often incongruent from the conversation. The case could be made that the child directed speech isn't aiding the development of language, and certainly, Grice would argue that it violates his maxim of relevance.

Chomsky would make the argument that the child would learn with minimal interaction from the caregivers. In utterances like when Jayce labels the "ball" and the "banana", he would argue that Jayce's LAD is telling him that his understanding of 'banana' is correct, and so he is regressing to his view on what a 'banana' is. Similarly, Piaget's cognitivist school of thought would agree with Chomsky, in the sense that Jayce has a cognitive deficiency in understanding the concept of a 'banana', but Jayce's LAD is dominant in convincing Jayce that he is correct. Whilst Chomsky's theory does explain such complexities as this, Chomsky is described as an "armchair linguist" (Tomasello) because his method is purely hypothetical and doesn't have any neuroscientific backing. However, case studies of feral children like Genie Wiley have proved that is near impossible for a child to learn language after the LAD's critical period, regardless of the use of CDS. This said, Bard and Sach's research into 'Jim' who had two deaf parents, proved that despite the 'interaction' with the TV, toys and other sources of language. 'Kim' was unable to acquire language, however, he eventually did manage to learn to speak, after the interaction with caregivers.

In conclusion, it can be argued that both child directed speech and nativist approach could both be responsible for a child's language development, and it is likely that a mix of both is the true key to the answer, but it is impossible to say for sure that either are a major factor.

Examiner comments:

AO1: Precise labelling, clear, guided argument, supported by examples. 13 marks.

AO2: Covers a range of issues, selectively. Key theories which are challenged. Evaluative with an individual overview. 14 marks.

Total mark: 27/30.

June 2018, question 5. Data and question available on the AQA website.
Without a doubt, being able to accurately convey your ideas and thoughts is a vital skill. Currently in the UK, the government sets guidelines on expected levels of accuracy called the 'NC levels'. These levels aim to assess children on their ability to write both accurately and for different contexts, as detailed by the work of Rothery, therefore academically, the view is absolutely right. However, there is also a need for a more creative approach where children can be rewarded for their attempts to be imaginative with both ideas and spelling.

Rickford would agree with the view, as he has theorised about the need for an accurate ability to write. He argues that there is a necessity for rules, and that children should learn these rules. For example, in Data Set 2, Iris has clearly learned the rules and conventions associated with writing a letter, like by starting her work by addressing the intended reader and by signing-off with her name and "lots of love". In addition, Rickford argues that children should be taught to write in dialect in order to directly enhance their ability. In spelling how words sound, the child may find it easier to learn to write and then to apply their knowledge elsewhere. For example in Data Set 3 Iris is struggling with the word 'fruit' which has no phoneme-grapheme correspondence. In particular, she is struggling with the /ui/ digraph which makes the /u:/ diphthong. Rickford may argue that Iris will then develop knowledge of sounds and their changing graphemes dependant on their place in the word.

Torrance has researched the impact of caregivers when correcting children. In the examples Iris is writing in the 'home' context and so isn't likely to get corrected in the same way that she would if she was in school. For example, Iris is yet to grasp, like many other children schwa in 'freezer'. She has a different phonological perspective to her MKOs, therefore a gap of knowledge which would need to be filled by a caregiver in order to close the zone of proximal development, as argued by Read and Vygotsky. Torrance would argue that if Iris was to be corrected, it would aid learning and accuracy, therefore supporting the need for the development of accuracy.

However, there is also the need for developing creativity, and some linguists have argued at length about the importance of creativity. For many children, learning to write is a challenging task, and can seem like, as Crystal describes, 'a jailhouse'. For Crystal, it is creative writing which offers 'the key' to the prison.

Maley and Abbot have argued that creativity acts as a release to the child. For example, whilst the piece isn't exactly what we would label as 'creative', Iris's recipe in Data Set 3 is something she feels compelled to write following her making ice cream and sorbet. It could be argued that Iris is finding her release in the form of writing inaccurately, but about something she enjoys. Maley and Abbot would certainly argue that it doesn't matter that the work is inaccurate because she is enjoying it.

In addition, pressure placed on the child to write accurately can have a serious negative impact on the child. Goouch and Lambirth studded the psychological impact of accuracy on a child and found that a child's self-esteem can suffer from being told they are wrong. This is especially true considering that Iris is only six years old and therefore is at a very impressionable time psychologically. It could be damaging for her if she was to learn to associate writing with being told she was wrong, regardless of the context.

However, there are many routes taken to help a child learn to write. This was detailed example, households in Roadville placed much less importance on accuracy, compared to Mainhouse, but all the children still managed to learn to write accurately and creatively. Therefore, it begs the question over whether it actually matters whether children develop their accuracy as a primary need or not. Personally, I believe that being accurate and creative are symbiotic – you cannot have one without the other. There will always be a need to be accurate, but we must try not to get so caught up in accuracy that we neglect creativity.

Examiner comments:
AO1: Precise labelling, clear, guided argument, examples less frequent in the second half. 12 marks.
AO2: Covers a range of issues, selectively. Key theories which are challenged. Evaluative with an individual overview. 14 marks.

Paper 2: Language Diversity and Change

The second exam is all about how language is diverse and how it has changed, but also, importantly, the attitudes people have towards these uses of language. It is 40% of your A-Level and is worth 100 marks.

Theory: Gender

The study of gender is divided into three key areas – dominance, difference and deficit.

The Dominance Model:

The Dominance model denotes the idea that men are more dominant in language. Here are some ideas which discuss this:

Name	Idea, concept and theory
Spender	Introduced the idea of 'male as norm' – women are extensions of men. For example, men are always introduced first (Mr and Mrs).
Schulz and Lakoff	Terms are marked (called **'marked terms'**) to female equivalent – usually using the suffix -ess and -ette, for example, 'hostess', 'bachelorette'.
Stanley	There are 220 negative terms to describe a promiscuous woman, but only 20 to describe an equivalent male.
Schulz	Terms used to describe women have become more negative over time. Schulz calls this **semantic derogation** or semantic degeneration, for example, 'spinster'.
Perrson	Animal insults are used to allude to a woman's sexual behaviour – usually to imply prostitution.
Parker et al	Commenting on a women's sexual behaviour is designed to damage her social status and cause negative psychological effects.
Holmes	Women are often referred to as food and animals, for example, 'cow', 'sugar'.

Zimmerman and West	Men interrupt women 96-100% of the time in mixed-sex conversations.
Beattie	Zimmerman and West's study wasn't accurate because their sample was far too small. Beattie's study uses 10 times as many participants and states that men and women interrupt with equal frequency.
Greif	Parents interrupt daughters more than sons and male parents interrupt more overall.
Fishman	Women are left to do the 'conversational shitwork' – if they do not do it, the conversation would fail.
Coates	Men control the topic of conversation and usually keep the topic to usually male-orientated subjects.
The Bechdel test	This judges whether a piece of work (book, film, theatre, TV etc) has: • Two women • Who talk to each other • About something other than men Many pieces of work fail this test!

The Deficit model:

This model looks at the idea that women's language is inherently weak. Here are the theories you can use:

Name	Idea, concept and theory
Lakoff	Lakoff believes that women's language contains many different features which make it weak. Here are just a few: • **Intensifiers/degree modifiers** – 'very', 'so', 'really'. • **Hedging** – expressing weak opinion – 'sort of'. • Avoiding swearing. • **Weak adjectives** – adjectives which contain a small value, for example, 'nice'. • **Back-channelling** – passively agreeing and supporting, for example, 'yeah', 'umhum'.
O'Barr and Atkins	Men use deficit language features in the courtroom. This suggests that it's more about powerless language than it is about gendered language.
Jesperson	Women's language is littered with non-fluency features because they speak before thinking. BUT, this is not a linguistic report – it's based on public perception.
ESRC	Women use 'fuck' 50 times more often than before 1990.

The Difference Model:

The Difference model believes that women and men communicate differently. Here are the theories you can use:

Name	Idea, concept and theory
Tannen	There are six different ways that men and women communicate differently: 1. **Advice vs understanding** – men will often try to fix a problem rather than understand the emotional needs. 2. **Conflict vs compromise** – women dislike being confrontational, whereas men do not mind this. 3. **Independence vs intimacy** – men prefer to be independent, whereas women prefer intimacy. 4. **Information vs feelings** – men will often only provide factual information, but many women take an emotional stance. 5. **Orders vs proposals** – men will often make commands where women will suggest. 6. **Status vs support** – men will try to be competitive to improve their status, but women will be seek reassurance and support.
Coates	All-male conversations are competitive whereas all-female conversations are co-operative.
Tannen	Male talk is **report-orientated** – they want to report the facts. Female talk is **rapport-orientated** – they do it to maintain friendships.
Cameron	Bitching is a part of female talk, but not male, because covertly dominant behaviour is more acceptable.
Pilkington	Male house talk is characterised by insults.
Howe	Men and women play different roles in conversation: • Men are active participants, keen to respond and provide their opinion. • Women are active listeners, responding through backchanneling.
Hyde	**The Gender Similarities Hypothesis:** There are more similarities between the genders than there is difference.

Theory: Regional, national and international varieties

Language differs depends on where you are from. This varies lexically, grammatically and phonologically.

Here are some key pieces of terminology you need to know:

- **Accent** – how you say something.
- **Dialect** – the words you use.
- **Matched guise** – an experiment where one speaker speaks in a range of different accents in order for people to pass a judgement about an accent.
- **Shibboleth** – a collection of features based on how language is used in a place.
- **G-dropping** – the word-final /g/ sound gets dropped.
- **H-dropping** – the word-initial /h/ sound gets dropped.
- **Yod-coalescence** – the pronunciation of the /j/ sound in words like Tuesday.
- **Received Pronunciation (RP)** – an accent which is typically described as 'posh' – it uses all the prestigious pronunciations. Its association with the Queen and the BBC lead it to be viewed as 'correct'. It is characterised by features like the long 'a' in words like 'bath', not dropping any letters or sounds and yod-coalescence. Only about 2% of the UK speak it.
- **Brummie** – speakers who using a Birmingham accent.
- **Glottal stop** – the missing out of the /t/ sound in words.
- **TH-fronting** – pronouncing the 'th' at the start of words as /f/. For example, 'fing' instead of 'thing'.
- **Rhotic accent** – pronounces the 'r' after vowels in words like 'car'.

Regional varieties of English:

Name	Idea, concept and theory
Giles	**Matched guise** experiment found that speaker of RP were judged as: • Intelligent • Trustworthy • Unfriendly • Unsociable
Kerswill	Through a process called **dialect levelling**, accents and dialects are becoming more and more similar.
Mugglestone	The number of RP speakers is decreasing.
Harrington	Over a period of 50 years, the Queen's speeches have been diverging from RP.
Giles and Powesland	**Psychology lecturer experiment:** The same lecture delivered two identical lecturers to two groups using RP and the Birmingham accent. They found that the Brummie speaker was rated as less intelligent and was rated less favourably overall.
Montgomery	RP is used in adverts for technical descriptions. Regional accents are used for other things, particularly food.
Harbridge	**Joke study:** Survey 4000 people to find the funniest accent. It concluded: • Brummie was the funniest. • Liverpudlian accent was the next funniest. • RP was the least funny.
Trudgill	The archaic forms of the second person pronouns, thee and thou, are still used in Yorkshire.
Mahoney et al	**Guilt experiment:** Students were played recordings of fake police interviews of suspects with different accents. Brummie accents were more likely to be judged as guilty.

Giles	Capital punishment study: Five groups of students were given information about capital punishment in five different ways – four were lectures from speakers with RP, Somerset, South Welsh and Brummie accents and the final group were given the written equivalent. Giles found that: <ul><li>The RP speaker and the written presentation were the most impressive.</li><li>Brummie was the least impressive.</li><li>The RP speaker and the written presentation were most likely to change the students' minds.</li></ul>
Rosewarne	Coined the term 'Estuary English' to describe the language of the people who lived near the Thames estuary. This variety contains the following variations: <ul><li>Phonological – there is a glottal stop, yod-coalescence, TH-fronting and h-dropping.</li><li>There are no notable lexical or grammatical differences.</li></ul>
Coggle	Estuary English acts a bridge between Cockney and RP.
Dent	Accents are like spoken birthmarks.

International varieties of English (Global English):

Name	Variety of English	Idea, concept and theory
GENERAL	American	American English contains a number of features which are different to British English: • **Lexical** – 'fall' instead of 'Autumn', 'candy' instead of 'sweets'. • **Grammatical** – '-t' can be added instead of '-ed' for past tense verbs. For example, 'learnt' instead of 'learned'. • **Phonological** – rhotic accent. • **Orthographical** - <er> digraph instead of <re>, simplification of spelling, like 'color' instead of 'colour'.
Webster	American	Wrote the 'Blue Back Speller' which was influential in **codifying** the American spelling system. His aim was to make the American English's orthography simpler and easier than British English so that there was **greater grapheme-phoneme correspondence.**
Engel	American	Hates Americanisms and claim that they are ruining British English. He believes that there is a huge identity issue with British English.
Murphy	American	The difference between British and American English is still very different and Americanisms enter Britain in the same way that British features enter America.
Pyles and Algeo	American	There is essentially no difference between American and British English – the differences are meaningless.
Algeo	American	American English is expanding British English, and this is a good thing.
Kim and Elder	American	Many American expressions are culturally dependent.
General	Australian	Australian English contains a number of features which are different to British English: • **Lexically:** 'digger for soldier'.

		• **Phonologically**: declarative statements end like interrogatives (high rising terminal), unstressed vowels turn to schwas. • **Grammatically**: collective nouns are treated as singular. For example, 'the sheep was eating' instead of 'the sheep were eating'.
General	African-American Vernacular English (AAVE)	**African-American Vernacular English** contains a number of features which are different to British English: • **Lexically**: 'Yo' is used as a greeting, 'homie' to refer to a friend. • **Phonologically**: 'th' sounds pronounced as /d/, g-dropping. • **Grammatically**: the copular verb does not exist. For example, 'the dog barking' instead of 'the dog is barking'. Frequent use of 'ain't'.
Kandiah	General	English's spread is a direct result of colonisation.
Crystal	General	Colonisation isn't the only reason for spread – the power associated with the countries who speak English furthers its spread.
Modiano	General	All varieties of English share a common set of factors at their hearts and then each variety has small individual changes.
McArthur	General	His model suggests that you can group different varieties of English together and this model does not give focus to any particular variety, showing them all as equal.
Graddol	General	English may lose its popularity as other languages become more dominant like Mandarin or Spanish.
Ostler	General	Technology will cause English to lose its prominence as translation software will be utilised.
Beneke	General	80% of all interactions in English are between non-native speakers.
Crystal	General	Different places adopt and adapt English to suit their needs.

Kachru	General	World Englishes can be modelled like this:
		Inner – English is the main language and it has a strong grounding. For example, UK, USA and Australia.
		Outer – English is present in this place because of colonisation. For example, India and Singapore.
		Expanding – English is used there but has not been placed there through invasion or colonisation. For example, China and Japan.
		The issue with this model is that it is somewhat elitist and that those varieties in the centre of the circle are better than other varieties.

In addition, to these theories, you can also find a number of theories for region in the social groups section. Including: Petyt, Labov and Trudgill.

Theory: Social groups

Social groups are groups of people who share a common characteristic. This may be age, gender, occupation, ethnicity, social class and more.

Here are some key terms you may need to know:

- **Expletives** – swear words.
- **Multiple negation** – using more than one negative in a sentence. For example, 'I ain't done nothing'.
- **Standard forms** – the socially accepted way of saying things (using Standard English).
- **Overt prestige** – a form of social value you get from using standard forms.
- **Covert prestige** – a form of social value you get from using non-standard forms.
- **Convergence** – language becomes more similar.
- **Divergence** – language becomes more different.
- **Code** – a form of language.
- **Genderlect** – the language of a gender.
- **Sociolect** – the language of a social group.
- **Ethnolect** – the language of an ethnic group.
- **Teenspeak** – the language of teenagers.
- **Polari** – a secret code used by gay men to communicate when homosexuality was illegal.

Here are some theories for writing about social groups:

Name	Social group	Idea, concept and theory
Eckert	Age	There are three forms of age: • **Chronological** – how long someone has been alive. • **Social** – how someone interacts socially, for example, like marriage and the birth of a first child. • **Biological** – physical maturity.

Parrott	Age	Teenage identity is characterised by: <ul><li>Rebellion</li><li>Forbidden behaviour</li><li>Exclusion</li><li>Idolisation</li></ul>
Stenstrom	Age	Teenspeak contains: <ul><li>Slang</li><li>Expletives</li><li>Contractions</li><li>Name calling</li><li>Insult battles</li></ul>
Eckert	Age	Teenspeak distances teenagers from adults.
Zimmerman	Age	Teenspeak is influenced by: <ul><li>Media</li><li>Music</li><li>Internet</li></ul>
DeKlerk	Age	Teenagers have the ability and freedom to challenge and adapt linguistic norms
Tagliamonte	Age	When communicating online, teenagers use more intensifiers. There is no evidence to suggest a decline in grammar.
Eckert	Age/gender	**Reading study:** Looked at children's use 9 different **non-standard forms** including multiple negation and 'ain't'. She linked this to whether they thought criminal activity was acceptable. Found that: <ul><li>Boys were more likely to approve of criminal activity</li><li>Those children who approved of non-standard forms were more likely to use non-standard forms</li></ul>

		• There is a link between the covert prestige of using non-standard forms and standard forms.
Eckert	Age	**Detroit study - Jocks and Burnouts:** Eckert studied two types of students in Detroit - Jocks and Burnouts. Jocks were highly engaged in school and Burnouts were less interested by it and often engaged immoral behaviour (like smoking and drinking). She studied **non-standard forms** and most notably **negative concord (multiple negation)**. She found that: • Jocks used almost all standard forms • Burnouts used predominantly non-standard forms • Importantly, it showed that those in the same social group spoke similarly.
Labov	Age	**Martha's Vineyard study:** Labov looked at inhabitants of the island of Martha's Vineyard. He noted that the younger members (who worked or studied there for some of the year) converged to the vowel pronunciation of the older members of the island when tourists arrived to distance themselves.
Labov	Social class	**New York stores study:** Labov looked at the presence of the **post-vocalic rhotic /r/** (the /r/ sound which comes after the vowel in words like part), which is a very prestigious pronunciation in New York. He compared the speech of sales assistants in 3 different stores of different classes by getting them to say 'fourth floor' and then repeat it. Here is what he found: • Klein's (working class) – used it the least.

		• Macy's (middle class) – wasn't overly used when first asked but used more when asked to repeat it. This shows that the assistants wanted to adapt their language to suit the class. • Saks (upper class) – used it the most.
Trudgill	Social class / gender	**Norwich study:** Trudgill was looking at the pronunciation of words which end with -ing. He was looking at whether the pronunciation had the **word-final /g/**. He asked participants to estimate how many times they used standard and non-standard forms and compared this to what they actually did. Here are the results: • The higher the social class, the lower the number of non-standard forms. • The lower the social class, the higher the number of standard forms. • Women of all classes reported higher usage of standard forms than they actually used. • Women used more standard forms than men. • Men of all classes reported higher usage of standard forms than they actually used. Therefore, social class influences language more than gender.
Petyt	Social class	**Bradford study:** People who were socially aspirational tried to pronounce words with the **/ʌ/ and /ʊ/** sounds in differently, like cushion. This led to them using the wrong vowel sound through hypercorrection. He also found that the lower the class a person was, the more likely they were to drop the **word-initial /h/** in words like 'house'.

Bernstein	Social class	**Restricted and elaborated code experiment:** Bernstein believes there are two types of **'code'** that can be used to communicate. **Restricted code** uses lots of **conjunctions, context-dependent language** and **non-standard syntax**. **Elaborated code** uses much more Standard English. His research found that: • Children of all classes understood both codes when it was spoken to them. • Working-class children speak using restricted code. • Middle-and-upper-class children speak using elaborated code predominantly but can use restricted code. • This disadvantages working-class children, as elaborated code is used in many formal situations.
Multicultural London English (MLE)	Ethnicity	There is a variety of English which started in London called **Multicultural London English (MLE)**. This variety is popular amongst young black teenagers. This contains the following features as examples: • **Lexical** – 'peng' (adjective meaning 'good') and 'creps' (noun meaning 'shoes'). • **Grammatical** – sentences may be constructed by starting 'why' and ending 'for' like, for example, 'why you eating that for?'. In addition, 'man' replaces the first-person singular pronoun (I). • **Phonological** – th-stopping – where the 'th' at the start of words becomes 't'. For example, 'thing' → 'ting'.

		There is no standard set of features of MLE – it varies depending on the location. The media often labels it 'Jafaican' due to its Jamaican roots.
Kerswill	Ethnicity	MLE will replace **Cockney Rhyming Slang (CRS)**.
Rampton	Ethnicity	MLE is spread through friendship groups.
Drummond	Ethnicity	MLE is a key part of the sociolect of young people in Manchester. Drummond has retitled MLE as **'Multicultural Urban British English' (MUBE)** which reflects its spread.
Khan	Ethnicity	Ethnicity was a central factor influencing a person's language.
Rampton and Harris	Ethnicity	There are four ways to categorise the view of ethnolects: 1. **Deficit** – there is something lacking. 2. **Difference** – there is nothing wrong with the variety, it's just different. 3. **Domination** – the variety should be oppressed. 4. **Discourse** – the previous three aren't correct – they are too simple – language, its community and its culture cannot be easily defined.
Leap	Sexuality	Coined the term **'Lavender linguistics'** to describe the study of language and sexuality.
Lakoff	Sexuality	Gay men adopt deficit features to mirror women's language.
Baker	Sexuality	The speech of gay people uses puns, acronyms and lexical items which only make sense to those in the community.
Kulik	Sexuality	You cannot tell someone's sexuality because of their language.
Butler	Sexuality/ gender	Your use of language and your behaviour can perform an identity. For example, gay men may choose to adopt feminine speech patterns to consciously be different from heterosexual men.

Theory: Occupation

This section turns its attention to how language is spoken in the workplace. Here are some key pieces of terminology:

- **Jargon** – language used which is specific to a certain area. For example, 'wings', 'lighting rig' and 'revolve' are all pieces of jargon used in theatre.
- **Hierarchy** – the structure of power within an institution
- **Phatic conversation** – conversation which fulfils a social function. Sometimes referred to as 'small talk'.
- **Legalese** – the language of law. A highly Latinate language and often very opaque to non-legal workers.

Here are the theories you need to know:

Name	Idea, theory and concept
Swales	Coined the term **'discourse communities'** to describe groups of people with a common goal/purpose who need language (as a form of communication.
Crystal	Use of jargon is part of an identity at work.
Drew and Heritage	Jargon makes the workplace efficient. For example, kitchens are quick-paced environments and so using jargon will help to ensure the job doesn't fall behind.
Spolsky	Using jargon shows you are part of the discourse community – however, not knowing it can make you feel like you do not belong.
Plain English Campaign	A group who campaign against jargon and argue that language which is transparent should be used.
Herbert and Straight	**Compliments** flow down the hierarchy from those in the highest position to those in the lowest.
Drew and Heritage	Occupational language has an **inferential framework** which is about how members have a shared way of communicating, thinking and behaving. In terms of language, this includes:

	<ul><li>**Enforced turn taking**</li><li>**Conversation which is goal-orientated**</li><li>**Asymmetry**</li><li>**Jargon**</li></ul>
Koester	A key part of workplace discourse is **phatic communication** – conversations can be either **transactional or interactional**.
Hornyak	Workplace conversations are usually initiated by the person with the most power.
Kim and Elder	Miscommunication between Korean and American colleagues was due to people not using agreed language.
Fairclough	Conversations are work are becoming more and more informal – this is called **conversationalisation**.
Sinclair and Coulthard	Teachers use the IRF structure in the classroom: <ul><li>**Initiation** – the teacher provokes an answer</li><li>**Response** – the child responds</li><li>**Feedback** – the teacher provides feedback</li></ul>
Holmes and Stubbe	When someone with power talks to someone with less power, they can decide to downplay or assert their authority.
French and Raven	There are fuve bases of power which a person may have: <ol><li>**Coercive** – the power to force someone to do something. Should they refuse, there would be some form of punishment.</li><li>**Expert** – knowledge and information which marks them as someone with power.</li><li>**Legitimate** – genuine power because of position.</li><li>**Reward** –the ability to reward a subordinate for complying.</li><li>**Referent** –a good rapport or a mutual respect with someone makes them want to comply.</li></ol>

Theory: Language Change

Here are the key pieces of terminology you need to know:

- **Prescriptivism** – belief that language should be prevented from changing.
- **Descriptivism** – belief that all language varieties are positive.
- **Archaic** – old and out-dated.
- **Political correctness** – avoiding language which could be deemed offensive.
- **Codification** – a change becomes officially recognised. For example, being added to a dictionary.
- **Strong verbs** – verbs which change when changing the tense. For example, 'swim' → 'swam'.
- **Weak verbs** – verbs which take an inflection when changing tense. For example, 'walk' → 'walked'.

Historical change:

Name	Type of change	Idea, concept and theory

GENERAL	Lexical	New words enter our language through the following processes:
		• **Lexical innovation** – using words we already have to form new ones
		  ○ **Affixation** – adding a prefix to an existing word. For example, 'Remainers'
		  ○ **Blending** – taking parts of two existing words. For example, 'Brexit'.
		  ○ **Clipping or abbreviating** – removing part of a word. For example, 'exam' instead of examination.
		  ○ **Conversion** – a word changes class. For example, 'email' – a change from a noun to a verb.

<table>
<tr>
<td></td>
<td></td>
<td>

- o **Compounding** – combining two existing words. For example, 'football'.
- o **Reduplication** – combining two similar sounds. For example, 'walkie-talkie'.
- o **Acronymisation and initialisation** – taking the first letters in phrases and forming a word. For example, 'BBC' and 'laser'.
- **Lexical invention** – using completely new words.
  - o **Borrowing/loan words** – new words are brought in from other languages. For example, 'Blitz' from German.
  - o **Eponymisation** – using someone's name to form a word. For example, 'to google' after the search engine.
  - o **Neologisation** – a completely new word is invented. For example, 'Mx' as a new pronoun.

</td>
</tr>
<tr>
<td>GENERAL</td>
<td>Semantic</td>
<td>

As time goes on, the meaning of words changes. Here is a list of processes of change:

- **Amelioration** – a word gains a more positive meaning, for example, 'dank'.
- **Bleaching** – a word loses power, for example, 'crap'.
- **Derogation** – a word gets a worse meaning over time. For example, 'spinster'.
- **Expansion** – a word's definition expands to cover more. For example, 'bird' used to refer to just small birds.
- **Metaphor and metonymy** – a word/phrase become a metaphor or metonym and so its meaning changes. For example, 'doghouse'.

</td>
</tr>
</table>

		• **Restriction** – a word loses some of its meanings. For example, 'gay' has lost its meaning of 'happy'. • **Neosemy** – a word gains a completely new meaning. For example, 'surf' the waves → 'surf' the internet.
Angles, Saxons and Jutes	Lexical	When they invaded, the Angles, Saxons and Jutes brought large amounts of their language within them and as such, imported lots of their language into Old English. Including: • Words for family • Verbs like 'drink' and 'go' • Prepositions
Vikings	Lexical and grammatical	The Vikings brought with them new words like 'sky', 'skull' and 'anger' and a **simplified grammatical system.**
Normans	Lexical	The invasion of the Normans and subsequent domination led to a huge amount of (Norman) French terms into the language, vastly increasing the Middle English lexicon.
Wycliffe	Lexical	Translated the Bible from Latin to English.
The Chancery	Lexical and orthographical	Decided to make English changes to **standardise** the use of English. For example, by removing the use of 'hath' and deciding to use 'I'.
Traditionalist campaigners	Orthographical	Wanted spelling to reflect the history of the language. This includes changing orthography to Latinate spellings. For example, adding the <h> in 'rhyme' to match 'rhythm'.
The Great Vowel Shift	Phonological	**Long vowel sounds** moved from the front of the mouth to further back. Some sounds also became **diphthongs**. For example, 'mouse' was originally pronounced as 'moose'.
Tyndale	Lexical	Translated the Bible, but with slightly more success than Wycliffe.

King James I	Lexical and grammatical	Ordered a Bible in English which was heavily **rhetorical**, so could be read out and used **archaic lexis** and **grammatical structures** to make it sound older and wiser.
Gutenberg	Orthographical	Invented the printing press.
Caxton	Orthographical	Brough the printing press to England. Made decisions on which spellings to use – orthography became more fixed.
Renaissance thinkers	Lexical	The rebirth of Greek and Latin ideas led to importation of many **Greek and Latinate lexis** into English.
The Inkhorn Controversy	Lexical	Concern was raised over the high numbers of lexis (**Inkhorn terms**) which were being imported from Latin and Greek.
Cawdrey	Lexical and orthographical	Wrote the first dictionary to provide terms and definitions. Aimed to try and fix orthography.
Shakespeare	Lexical	Shakespeare introduced over 400 new words into English.
Johnson	Lexical and orthographical	Published a dictionary in 1755 containing 40,000 words and provides spellings. However, there is some controversy over the terms he chose not to include and his definitions are biased. He sought to provide 'regulation', though admits that trying to control language is like trying to 'lash the wind'.
Swift	Lexical	Thought that English needed to be corrected, improved and ascertained. He felt it was being destroy. He disliked: • Contractions • Long words • New words • Borrowed words • Clipped words

		• Young people changing language
Académie Francais	Lexical and grammatical	Worked to accept or reject additions into the French language and to preserve grammar.
Lowth	Grammatical	Wrote an influential grammar book for teaching in which he stated (among other things) that **multiple negation** wasn't acceptable in English as two negatives in Maths make a positive. Importantly, this was his own personal opinion, but has become codified.
Murray	Grammatical	Believed that we shouldn't use **split infinitives**. For example, it should be 'to walk proudly' rather than 'to proudly walk'.
The Industrial Revolution	Phonological	The rise in industry caused mass migration and so new regional accents began to develop. For example, the Liverpudlian accent stems from Irish migration.
The British Empire	Lexical	The British Empire started colonising and acquiring new words from places they visited.

Technological change:

Name	Idea, concept and theory
General	Over the course of the past 30 years, the increases in technology have been vast. The internet and SMS messages allowed communication to be digital. This led to new varieties of English emerging to meet this new medium. Limits on characters encouraged users to be innovative with language and therefore, speed and length became a factor in language composition. This was seen in the changes in **orthography**: • **Abbreviations** – for example, 'cuz'. • **Numerical-phonetic substitution** – replacing words or sounds with numbers - for example, 'wuu2' uses the number '2' instead of the word 'to'. • **Initialisms** – for example, 'lmao'. • **Acronyms** – for example, 'lol'. • **Emoticons and emojis** – for example, '☺' and ':-)' • **Non-standard punctuation** – for example, 'No way!!!'
Carrington et al	Text language is a form of **linguistic compression**.
Werry	Text language users often use more letters in order to accommodate **tone**, **intonation** and **paralinguistic features**.
Shortis	Text language shows creativity.
Crystal	Text language is just the next stage in English's evolution.
McWhorter	Text language allows users to write how they speak, and this is a miracle change.
Wood	There is no link between the use of text language and use of standard forms.
Tagg	It is more likely to find unintentional spelling mistakes than it is to find text language.
Lee	The more intensive a texter, the smaller their vocabulary.
Cingle and Sundar	Use of text language is linked to lacking an understanding of grammar.
Fairclough	Computers mirror actual conversation, like with turn taking.

Tagliamonte	Teenagers use of instant messaging and emails can help us to predict how we will be using language in spoken interactions.
Shortis	The internet allows users to create an identity which isn't real.

Modelling change:

Aitchison	You can categorise prescriptivist views in three ways: • **Crumbling castle view** – English was once a thing of beauty and is now being ruined. • **Damp spoon syndrome** – changes to language are a result of laziness and disrespect. Stems from the idea of putting a damp spoon in a bowl of sugar. • **Infectious disease assumption** – change spreads like a plague, it should be avoided.
Hitchings	All prescriptivist views are proxy arguments for something else.
Halliday	**Functional theory:** Language changes because the needs of its speakers need it to change. For example, when there were lots of new things being invented in terms of technology, we needed new words, so we invented them. This only accounts for lexical change, however. In addition, it shows that we can direct change, but not control it.
Hockett	**Random fluctuation theory:** We make mistakes in language and these mistakes become codified. For example, smartphones often correct 'fuck' to 'duck. However, if this it to be believed, it does not explain how similar changes occur in different languages.
Pinker	**Euphemism treadmill:** As a euphemism stops being used, a new euphemism arrives to replace it. This is a constant cycle.
Substratum theory	This theory states that language changes primarily through contact with other countries. However, this cannot account for all changes.
Lexical gaps theory	This theory states that new words enter our language where there is a space for it when we need to express something. For example, when a wireless internet was invented, there was a gap for naming it.

Bailey	**Wave model:** A change starts in geographical centre and ripples out geographically. The closer you are to the centre, the quicker you will adopt the change.
Trudgill	Challenges the 'wave model' – argues that often smaller villages and towns get missed out of these changes as they spread from city to city.
Chen	**The 's-curve' model:** This model looks at how changes move from inception to mass usage.

At 1 – the change is new and only in use amongst social groups.
At 2 – the change has gained some traction and there are a few people using it now.
At 3 – many people are now using the change.
At 4 – everyone who is going to adopt the change is now using it. This is never going to be everybody as people will always resist change.

An example of this change would be 'Brexit'. Initially, only experts were using the term (1), then the media started using it (2). This caused mass public usage (3) and eventually, almost all of the UK is now using it (4).

Aitchison	Language change is a process of **PIDC**:
	• **Potential** – there is room for a change
	• **Implementation** – the change takes place

	• **Diffusion** – the change spreads • **Codification** – the change becomes recognised. For example, by being added to the dictionary.
Crystal	**Tide metaphor:** Language change is like the tide washing on a beach. The tide will sometimes wash things ashore – sometimes these things stay for a long time and sometimes they will be washed away again. This is just like changes made to the language.

Exam walkthrough

Section A

The first section of the exam is entitled 'Language Diversity and Change' and gives you the choice of two questions – you must answer **ONE** of these. It is worth 30 marks and assesses AO1 for 10 marks and AO2 for 20 marks.

One of the biggest pitfalls for students answering this question is not planning their answer – it is extremely important to plan your answer! A quick 5-minute plan makes a huge difference on your essay as it allows you to know the direction you are taking your essay. You can read more about planning at the end of this section.

This section of the exam is BYOD – bring your own data! Which means that you will have to come prepared with some examples of language. For example, you should have some examples of occupational language and pieces of slang. You should use this data to support any point you are making.

Question 1

This question will be a language diversity question. This means the following areas could be assessed:

- **Gender**
- **Occupation**
- **Region**
- **Global English/World Englishes**
- **Social groups**

Or, you may be asked a more general question which allows you to take the essay in the direction which best suits you and your knowledge. Below, there are a set of practice questions you can attempt, if you wish. This book also contains a selection of essay titles and ready-made essay plans for you to read! The best answers will structure essays differently depending on the theory available, as you will be able to see.

The best answers on this question see language as varied and subject to lots of variation. You may want to consider attitudes to different types of language in your answer, though this should always be linked to the question and the argument that you are making.

Question 2

This question will be a language change question. This means the following areas could be tested, though this is not an exhaustive list:

- **Language decay**
- **Language control**
- **Standardisation**
- **Technology**
- **Language spread and diffusion**

In order to be prepared to answer a Language Change question, think carefully about **HOW** language has changed and, crucially, **WHY** language has changed. Think about the attitudes which are behind actions and how prescriptivism and descriptivism play a part in things. For more help on this, you can look at some of the essay plans at the end of this section!

To structure your essays, you should use the following key sections:

PROVE
- This section is all about proving to the examiner you know what they are asking you.
- Underline the key words in the question.
- Define the key terms in your introduction.
- Write about the debate or issue the question highlights.
- Indicate you know the direction of your essay.

SUPPORT
- You should have 1-3 of these paragraphs.
- Use a theory to support the statement.
- Support that theory with another theory.
- Back the theory up with some data you can think of.
- If you can, you could challenge this point with another theory.

REFUTE
- You should have 1-3 of these paragraphs.
- Use a theory to refute the statement.
- Support that theory with another theory.
- Back the theory up with some data you can think of.
- If you can, you could challenge this point with another theory.

CONCLUDE
- Your essay is not a mystery novel – there should be no surprises at the end!
- Summarise what you have argued.
- State clearly what you think – try not to sit on the fence, take a side!

Section B

The second section of this exam is entitled 'Language discourses' and is worth 70 marks in total. This section will assess your ability to respond to ideologies and attitudes to language, as well as your ability to write creatively.

Question 3

This question is the biggest question in your exams. It is worth 40 marks and assesses **AO1** for 10 marks and **AO3** and **AO4** for 15 marks each.

This is a textual analysis question and you will be given two extracts from sources which contain an attitude about language. The topic will be something from language diversity and change, but will not necessarily be an exact topic you have studied. Both texts will be on the same topic, but they may not have the same viewpoint. For example, text A may present positive or descriptivist views and text B may present negative or prescriptivist views. Though, you may find that they both have the same attitude. Once you have read through the articles, you should try to label them as having a certain viewpoint, for your own benefit.

To show your examiner you understand the issue at the heart of the texts, you should start your answer by using the following sentence:

> Both of the texts contain discourses of (language discourse) and they approach the matter in similar/different ways.

There are many different types of language discourses you could use in that gap – these could be, but are not limited to:

- **Linguistic purity** – the writer believes that there is a pure form of language and what they're writing about IS or ISN'T this form.
- **Linguistic control** – the writer believes language can/can't/should/shouldn't be controlled.
- **Linguistic inferiority or superiority**– the writer believes that certain forms of language are better than others.

- **Linguistic decay and deformity** – the writer believes that language is in a state of decline or that a language variety isn't right.

Just as with Paper 1's questions on textual analysis, you are still required to look at representation and language, though you should try stay focused on the linguistic issues which is the topic of the article and look in depth at the language being used to represent it. However, there is an additional element required in question – comparison. You should look at how the two texts are similar or different in their language and the way they are representing things. Here is an adapted frame which may help you:

> Within text A, (thing being represented) is represented as (adjective). This is being done through the use of (language feature), for example "QUOTE". This is significant because... (link to context). This is a similar/different way to how text B is representing (thing being represented), as they are representing it as (adjective), using language like (language feature) in "QUOTE". This similarity/difference is significant because...

Here is what this may look like all put together:

> Both texts contain discourses of linguistic clarity but approach the matter in different ways. Within text A, jargon is represented as opaque. It is being represented like this through the use of the range of pre-modifying attributive adjectives like "impenetrable" and "confusing". The article has a pattern of using adjectives within this semantic field in order to create an overall representation of jargon to the reader. This is different to text B which is representing jargon as a useful piece of language to enable employees to communicate efficiently with each other. In contrast, their adjectives are very positive like "helpful" and "handy" in order to accentuate jargon's positive attributes. This difference is quite significant as the representations are contrasting, though text A is designed for the public and therefore positions jargon as being an enemy of the general public whereas text B is designed for employees and therefore positions jargon as being useful to the general public.

As with all the questions, **you MUST plan your answer** to this question. I have given an example of how to plan at the end of this section.

It is very important that when you are writing, you must always link language with context and then link the other text – this allows you to tackle all three assessment objectives. Often candidates forget one of the three and performing poorly on one often means that the others suffer as a direct result. You should also make sure you try to include the following forms of context:

- Technological
- Cultural
- Social
- Journalistic

Question 4
This question is worth 30 marks and is assessed by AO2 for 20 marks and AO5 for 10 marks. The question will ask you to produce a piece of writing.

This is a 'directed writing' task, which means you will have to produce a piece of writing which the exam board will specify. Whilst I cannot tell you what form of writing you are going to be asked for, the requirements of the task will be the same:

- You will need to write engagingly.
- You will need to write for non-specialists (i.e. people who have never studied A-Level English Language).
- You will need to engage with text A and B from question 3.
- You will need to include theory.

The topic of the writing will be based on the topic of the texts from question 3. A good way to think of this task is as a different way of writing an essay.

If you are asked to write an article, you may write it using the following format:

Headline

Standfirst

Introduction

Content

Conclusion

There are a number of guides you can use to help you write these:

- Your headline should have some relation to what you are writing about – if possible, there should be some intentional use of language, like a pun or alliteration.
- Your standfirst should be two sentences. The first should be about the topic area and the second should be about you.
- Your introduction should contain an anecdote or a key image which is relevant to the topic and should sum up a little bit about what you are going to talk about.
- Your content should do the following:
  - Explain 3-4 theories and how they are relevant – remember the person reading this wouldn't know any of this research.
  - Explain key terminology.
  - Make clear any debates in the area.
  - Make a direct reference to the texts you've read **BUT DO NOT CALL THEM TEXT A AND TEXT B.**
  - Have an opinion.
- Your conclusion should summarise what you have spoken about and then finally return to the anecdote or image from your introduction.

Here is what this may look like:

Last Christmas, accent you my heart

Accents are slowly losing some of their distinctiveness and those special little features which makes them so unique. Linguist, Tom Hollins investigates what is happening to our accents.

I love Christmas for a number of reasons – presents, food and, most importantly, family. When I get to see my family at Christmas, I always find it fascinating to listen to how we all say words differently. We're from all over the United Kingdom and so we all have our own special ways of talking – linguists call these 'shibboleths'. When I sat back and listened, it was great to hear the eclectic mix of sounds radiate around the room.

This article would go on to discuss the debates, issues and attitudes facing accents and then return to the image of Christmas and accents in the conclusion.

Here are some useful phrases which may help you when writing your answer:

- 'What linguists call...'
- 'This is called...'
- 'The technical term for this is...'
- 'Linguist, Robin Lakoff, has argued...'
- 'Language guru, David Crystal, believes...'
- 'This is hotly debated topic in linguistics...'
- 'I recently read an article by (TEXT A/B author) ...'
- 'Not all linguists agree with this, however...'

Exam timings

The exam lasts a total of **2 hours and 30 minutes**.

You should split your time as follows:

- **45 minutes on question 1/2**
  - **5 minutes planning.**
  - **35 minutes writing.**
  - **5 minutes checking your answer.**
- **1 hour on question 3**
  - **15 minutes annotating and planning.**
  - **40 minutes writing.**
  - **5 minutes checking your answer.**
- **45 minutes on question 4**
  - **5 minutes planning.**
  - **35 minutes writing.**
  - **5 minutes checking your answer.**

ANY TIME LEFT SPARE SHOULD BE USED TO CHECK YOUR ANSWERS

You may find it quite useful to write the timings on your exam paper at the start. For example, if the exam starts at 9AM, you would write:

9 - planning
9:05 – Q1/2
9:40 – checking
9:45 - reading and annotating texts/planning
10:00 – Q3
10:40 – checking
10:45 – planning Q4
10:50 – Q4
11:25 – checking

Doing this means you have very clear goalposts and you won't spend too long on any question.

Example exam questions

Language diversity – Evaluate the idea that…

- Men and women speak differently
- Women's language is inherently weak
- Men and women use language for different purposes
- A person's language can reveal their gender
- Women's language is characterised by prestigious forms
- The language of social groups is designed to exclude others
- A person's social network determines how they speak
- People of different ages speak different varieties of English
- Social groups do not impact on a person's language
- A social group is the most important factor which influences the use of language
- Occupational language should be transparent
- Jargon is a negative feature of occupational language
- Those who have the most power use language differently
- A person's occupation is the biggest influence on their use of language
- Workplace conversations are always transactional
- A person's region completely determines how they speak
- Local accents should be cherished
- Local accents are inferior to Received Pronunciation
- Global varieties are more similar than different
- Language forms a person's identity

Language change – Evaluate the idea that…
- Language change is characterised by deterioration
- Language is on a downwards spiral of informalisation
- Technology drives language change
- Language change imposed by authority is ineffective
- Politically correct language is a negative force
- It is impossible to control how language changes
- Language is always changing
- Language is changing quicker now than before

Model essay plans

'Evaluate the idea that men and women speak different'.

Prove:

- Give examples of how men and women speak differently.
- Mention Tannen and Lakoff.

Support:

- Tannen's difference model.
- Lakoff – women speak differently because their language is weak.
- Coates – conversation is different.

Refute:

- Challenge Lakoff with O'Barr and Atkins.
- Hyde – gender similarities.
- Sexuality – there is more difference inside genders than between.

Evaluate:

- Yes – they do speak differently.
- But difference is trivial and insignificant.

'Evaluate the idea that the language of social groups is designed to exclude others'.

Prove:

- Define social group.
- Examine – exclusion. Example, teenspeak.

Support:

- Parrott and Eckert on teenspeak.
- Link Stenstrom's examples of features of teenspeak and how these exclude. E.g. lmao.
- Identity – Martha's Vineyard.

Refute:

- Bernstein – working class children has not choice.
- MLE is a way of communicating rather than a means of communication.

Evaluate:

- Overall, yes.
- However, this may not always be about excluding or even designed that way.

'Evaluate the idea that occupational language should be transparent'.

Prove:

- Define occupational language.
- Examples of occ lang like jargon.
- Define transparency and introduce why this is an issue.

Support:

- Spolsky – can mark members as not part of the groups.
- Plain English Campaign – link doctors using jargon as an example.

Refute:

- Drew and Heritage – efficiency.
- Swales – part of community.
- Spolsky – can be useful to exclude people.

Evaluate:

- No – occupational language is designed to be opaque.
- Workplace runs better with it.

'Evaluate the idea that a person's location completely determines how they speak'.

Prove:

- Prove that regional variation exists – give a lexical, phonological and grammatical example.
- Debate about how much this influences.

Support:

- Dent – spoken birthmark.
- Trudgill – Yorkshire.
- Link shibboleths.

Refute:

- Other factors – e.g. social group. Link Labov's Martha's Vineyard study.
- Petyt – Bradford – social class.
- MLE has spread to other locations (Ives).

Evaluate:

- Overall, no.
- Plays a part, but not completely determinate.

'Evaluate the idea that it is impossible to control how language changes'.

Prove:

- Define language control .
- Give examples.
- State that some people try to control it.

Support:

- Johnson – lash the wind.
- Random fluctuation (Hockett).
- Swift's failure.
- Technology.

Refute:

- Codification – Lowth.
- Printing press.
- Political correctness.

Evaluate:

- Overall, yes.
- It is very difficult to gain some control over language change.
- Attempts are usually ineffective.

Model essays

June 2018, question 1. Question available on the AQA website.

British Standard English has spread around the world and formed new, different varieties of English. As English spreads further and further, the less similar the language becomes to the original British. For many, British Standard English (BSE), as it was the original form, holds the most prestige as a form of English. We define British Standard English as being the accept forms of use of English in Britain. Such varieties exist like, for example, in South African English, they use different lexis like 'robot' instead of 'traffic light'. In African-American Vernacular English (AAVE), their negation grammar is different, fronting the negative in phrases like 'no me go to the shops'. In addition, in AAVE, they use g-dropping in phrases like 'writing' to form 'writin' forming a /ŋ/ sound instead of a /ng/ sound.

The spread has caused the prestige of English to grow, with many countries using it as a compromise language in meetings where there the first language isn't the same. Research conducted by 'The Guardian' earlier this year discovered that English (in all its varieties) is the world's 'favourite' language. In South Africa, the denomination of English they use has connotations of power, authority and government, showing the high levels of prestige they hold English with.

Within the UK, there isn't always the view that BSE is superior, for example in Cheshire's study of girls and boys in a playground in Reading. She discovered that the use of non-standard forms, for example, using the past perfect verb 'was' instead of past progressive verb 'were' in sentences like 'we were going to the shop' was linked to the idea of covert prestige. This is a pattern, as in Detroit, Eckert found that the 'burnouts' – students who were more anti-social, were more likely to use multiple negation (or negative concord) in order to gain a greater level of peer group covert prestige. Although these aren't both from the use of BSE, it does demonstrate that Standard English isn't always a superior form. However, there is the counter-argument to be made with the idea of linguistic determinism (Sapir-Whorf hypothesis), with the idea that using a standard form, like BSE, is use of good language and that good language determines good thought.

The issue with varieties of English becomes complicated when we examine countries in Modiano's expanding circle. These countries, for example, Japan (denoted satirically as Engrish), have had no political or conflict-based involvement with Britain (or America) and thus, their use of English is particularly interesting. As Modiano notes, the issue with these varieties of English is that they are learning English from speakers who are not, themselves, speakers of BSE or ASE (American Standard English), and therefore, the quality of English declines. For example, speakers of Japanese English use 'erection' instead of 'election' in a complete mis-use of English.

Perhaps the most common variety of English used is in America, where the discovery of America led to the changing of BSE to suit the needs of the Americans, using lexis borrowed from the natives like 'racoon'. This is an example of what Crystal describes as the 'adopt and adapt' of world Englishes. Each place that adopts English will adapt it to suit the needs of the speakers. As they adapt the language, it becomes further and further from BSE. This has been modelled in many ways, such as Kachru's concentric circle model which places BSE in the inner circle and has other varieties moving around it. This has been challenged by Modiano whose model place shared language features at the centre of the circles, as all languages share commonalities.

It depends on what extent you value BSE. Prescriptivists like Engel who believes that American English is threatening BSE, value BSE as the standard and measure every other variety against it, in which case, BSE is always going to appear more superior. Often arguments about BSE being superior, as Hitchings suggests, are proxy issues for other issues. If however, you value BSE as simply the starting point, you can take the view that none of the varieties are any better than the other – they are all unique in their own ways.

Examiner comments:

AO1: Precise and detailed. Has an argument. Reader-guided throughout. Enjoyable to read. 10 marks.

AO2: Explores specific local factors leading to diversification. Good range of examples (phonologically, grammatically and lexically) and varieties. Conceptualised discussion. 18 marks.

Total mark: 28/30.

June 2018, question 3. Data and question available on the AQA website.
Both texts discuss issues surrounding politically correct language, tapping into contemporary discourse ideas of linguistic cleansing. Both texts think PC is a bad thing and is restricting the world in which we live in. The texts do not equivocate on their opinions – in both texts, the headline (A) and title (B) very clearly states their viewpoint. In text A, the use of the "=" symbol immediately equates political correctness with, quite seriously, the abstract noun phrase "language thought and control". The noun "control" suggests that those with power are restricting those inferior to them. This is especially true when considering that it is premodified with "language and thought", constricting free communication. Similarly, in text B, the noun phrase "the awful truth" hyperbolises the actual issue at hand. The pre-modifying adjective "awful" suggesting that it is somewhat of a tragedy.

Text A has a large focus on freedom, which is not surprising when considering the context in which it is written. The text, being American (indicated by American lexis like "theater")s, attacks freedom because of how Americans regard the importance of freedom. It is one of their core values, for example, the importance they place on the 4th July celebrations. The various forms of 'freedom' are repeated throughout the text, forming a pattern of conjoining the idea of political correctness destroying our sense of freedom. This is significant because aspects of the cultural context of both the intended reader and the author are working together to alter the way in which the text portrays the issue. In text B, however, it plays on the idea that British people use language. For example, it attacks terms of endearment like "dear" and "duckie", as a way of making the impact of political correctness personal to the reader.

The way in which the texts represent the issue is different. Within text A, the writer cohesively forms an argument about political correctness, using discourse markers like "firstly" to signify a flow of argument and guide the reader through the text. Additionally, the third point raise has the parenthesised subordinate clause "and most importantly" in order to signify to the reader that the argument's strongest issue. In doing this, the piece is trying to convince the reader that the writer's opinion is fact. The declarative mood used consistently throughout the piece forms a pattern in simple sentences like "political correctness is language control". Within text B, the argument is strengthened through the use of satire in the "THE A-Z" accentuates the list and draws the reader into it. The use of "A-Z" implies that this is the definitive list of terms, which represents the website as knowledgeable. This is then undermined through the use of the comedic terms like "common sense" creating a parallel between the ridiculousness of the PC and of anybody being offended by "common sense".

The texts illuminate the ways in which the different countries approach views about political correctness, culturally. Within text A, the argument acts as a proxy for issues surrounding power and freedom. The real issues isn't to do with the language people use, it's about the power of the so-called "manipulators" have to change the way people speak and think. Culturally, the American people are quite concerned with the power of those in authority, as seen in Donald Trump's election promise to 'take back control'. In contrast, in Text B the argument about mild inconvenience of British people having to use different terms to describe things. Culturally, British people like to reflect on how things were and so the aim of the piece is to remind British people about how things used to be, they are now and scaremonger about how it will be.

Examiner comments:

AO1: Describes; abstract noun, noun phrase, adjectives, discourse markers, parenthesis, declaratives, simple sentences. Thorough discussion of cohesion. 9 marks.

AO3: Evaluates discourse of freedom. Explores wider cultural contexts. 14 marks.

AO4: Evaluates different discourses. Compares significance of wider cultural contexts. 13 marks.

Total mark: 36/40.

June 2018, question 4. Data and question available on the AQA website.

Is our language Nineteen-Eighty-Flawed?

We live in a world increasingly consumed by being 'politically correct', and in danger of becoming exceedingly close to Orwell's 'newspeak'. Tom Hollins investigates what's wrong with our language.

It's not very often you get to turn on the TV and not hear about the latest issues surrounding people not being politically correct (i.e. using language that is appropriate for those you are describing). It was always splendid to see a clip of everyone's favourite racist, Nigel Farage banging on about 'political correctness gone mad', after his latest slur against women/ immigrants/ foreigners has caused outrage. The question is, what is wrong with our language?

The best way to look at political correctness is to examine the language we use to talk about women. Nobody can deny that feminism has come on leaps and bounds in the past few decades. We've seen many-a glass ceiling smash and with that, the removal of many words and phrases from our language that are deemed as 'not politically correct'. Linguist Janet Holmes has done extensive research into the way in which we refer to women (or more critically, how men speak to women). Her research detailed that there are 'semantic field' (linguist speak meaning a group of words connected by a common theme) of food and animals for the way in which women are referred to. For example, it would be absolutely unacceptable for a man to refer to a woman as 'tasty' or a 'bitch'. This issue has been debated by linguists heavily and begs the question as to how our language became so sexist.

You may have noticed that slowly, some of our words have started to become more neutral – for example, there are no more actresses in theatre – only actors. Linguistic dream-tream, Schulz and Lakoff have investigated this and found that the '-ess' suffix (ending to a word) marked the term as being female, and that over time, these terms have gained negative connotations (linguists call this 'semantic derrogation'). I was recently reading the 'political correctness – the awful truth' website and noticed that they complain about the 'banning' of the use of the term 'businessman' because of its marked difference between a man and woman. I'm not sure about you, but I would certainly argue that the only 'awful' thing about it all is that they exist in the first place...

The issue with words like 'businessman' is that they act as if men are the norm, an idea passionately presented by Dale Spender. Her work has been highly influential in the exploration of the formation of our language and is particularly insightful in this case. However, her work has been challenged by fellow linguist (and so-called feminist) Robin Lakoff. Lakoff claims that women are all-round weaker, and so have accepted a linguistically weaker position. Her argument, however, is often disputed by linguists because her research lacks evidence and her ideas are just her casual observations.

There you have it. Our political correctness masks out sexist language, and although it can be annoying, seeks to do more good than harm. In controlling our language, we are creating a more equal world. So next time Mr Farage is in hot water, remind yourself that he belongs there – there is no place for those who think that being politically correct is a bad thing in our new and equal society.

Examiner comments:

AO2: Classifies and characterises views. Evaluates views. Explores examples. Not fully focused on PC language and ideas – more on representation. 14 marks.

AO5: Transforms ideas relevantly, for audience showing significance. Excellent headline and well-written piece. 10 marks.

Total mark: 24/30.

Non-Exam Assessment (NEA): Language in Action

Original Writing

The original writing coursework is worth 50 marks and weights 10% of your overall grade. It takes the form of one of three forms of writing: persuasion, storytelling and information. You should choose a piece of writing which is around 750 words and covers one (or more) of these. Here are some ideas of what you could do:

- Speech
- Letter(s)
- Short story
- Children's story
- Rewritten ending
- Sequel to an existing novel
- Website
- Leaflet
- Article
- Travel writing
- Blog post
- Script for an audio tour

In addition to your writing, you should find a style model – this is a piece of writing completed by someone else which you can use to guide you. It could be linked by topic or genre, but shouldn't be exactly the same. For example, if you're writing an article on camping, you may use a piece of writing based on a story about camping. You should annotate your style model using the methods of analysis you have learned – you can refer to earlier in the book to help you with this. You will need to submit your annotated style model with your finished piece of writing.

In addition, you will also need a commentary. This is a piece of writing which will show the examiner how you have crafted your writing. It should be approximately 750 (excluding quotations) and should have direct references to your style model. Here are some questions to consider when writing your commentary:

- Why did I use that word?
- What structural devices did I use?
- What changes did I make over various drafts? Why did I make them?
- How is this similar to my style model?
- Why did I change this from my style model?
- How is my style model different from my writing? Why have I made changes?
- How does my piece fit with the genre?
- Why did changing X to Y make a difference? Why was it more effective?

Both your writing and commentary will be marked out of **25**, giving a total mark out of **50**.

Example Original Writing

This student decided to produce a piece of work in the style of the 'A letter to' section of the Guardian.

A Letter To... My Family - Seven years and now you know I'm gay

Seven years ago, I would never have dreamed pen would touch paper to write this daunting letter. Seven years ago, I became an 'Ethan' none of you knew. Seven years ago, I found the real me.

If I'm honest, I don't know if these words will ever meet your loving eyes; however, if they do, you should know the decision to write this letter was the hardest decision of my life and wasn't made lightly. You see, who you are to the world is pretty frightening, because what if the world doesn't like you? Yet, who I am to you is even more frightening, because what you think of me matters most of all.

For seven years now, I've hidden a part of myself from you – not because I'm ashamed, but because I'm scared. Scared of how you'll react and scared of how you'll feel about me. Part of me wants to hold onto who I've always been, because once you know this, you'll know everything about me... and that scares me too. The sacrifice of my personal silence for your pride has been worth every heart wrenching second: until now. Now I know that I can never truly be happy unless I am free of the huge burden this secret has been to me.
I am gay.

AND I WAS BORN THIS WAY

This is not a phase. It is part of who I am; just like being autistic or having brown hair.

AND I AM HAPPY...

...but I haven't always been. It destroyed me every day for those painful seven years because I never chose this. I would ask myself, why me? Why do I have to suffer the consequences of being different. My life slowly morphed into a musical of its own, singing and dancing my way through a script belonging to the straight character inside of me, my lines became routine, but that wasn't really me.

And inside me, my heart cries when I realise that you never truly knew the funny, caring, outgoing Ethan everyone knew at school. When I arrived home every day, it was like crossing an invisible line at the front door; entering the stage once again, prepared to give an Oscar-winning-performance.

We were on holiday together at Scarborough Beach when there was a moment, a subtly powerful moment, where my thoughts came crashing through my mind like the raging waves pounding beneath my feet. The destructive force of the new-found knowledge that I was gay weighed heavy on my shoulders. However, pain wasn't the only feeling that day. I felt relief too. The constant pressure on my mind had finally been lifted, I accepted who I was for the first time. Will you ever know that feeling too?

The toys you keep for my future grandchildren will stay untouched for eternity, and I am sorry. Esther will never get the biological chance to be an aunty, and I am sorry. I will never fulfil your hopes for the future of my life, because there will be no white picket fences or perfect bride, I am sorry.

In the wise words of Anthony Venn-Brown, an author who advocates LGBT rights - "Every single courageous act of coming out chips away at the curse of homophobia". By coming out to you, I hope to broaden your knowledge of the world a little more, show you that being gay isn't a bad thing, teach you that being different is okay and most of all prove to you that unconditional love for your child cannot be bent, altered or changed by a simple thing like me being gay.

Life is too short to lie to my own family. There is no greater agony than bearing an untold story inside of you. None. That is why this secret can no longer be kept hidden – love me or hate me I must live my life for me and I deserve to be happy in my own skin.

So, Mum, Dad and Esther, as the curtain lifts on my secret life I can only leave you with these parting words. Seven years ago, I would have never dreamed pen would touch paper to write this daunting letter. Seven years ago, I became an 'Ethan' none of you knew. Seven years ago, I found the real me... and now you know that 'me'.

This scored 24/25.

Example commentary

My chosen style model, "A Letter to... a universe that keeps sending me the wrong man" is from the 'Letter To' section of The Guardian and details the opinion of a girl who desires a perfect relationship, but never gets it. My own 'letter to' discloses my homosexuality to my family and, like my style model, desires a positive outcome, in the form of acceptance. However, unlike my style model, is less fatalistic, since I do not wish to present being gay as something inevitably ending in tragedy. The audience of the letter is ostensibly my nuclear family, though as it is unlikely they will read this and know it is from me, the audience is more likely to be Guardian readers; therefore, my stylistic devices were not only aiming to be emotive, but also aimed to entertain and inform readers of my experiences, much like my style model.

Because some audiences will find it hard to relate to the subject, my intentions were to use linguistic devices to enable them to feel the emotions I felt. My style model helped when planning the perspective my piece should be written from. Common of the 'Letter To' genre, the writer uses first person singular pronouns: "After 'I' waited you finally threw me one", coupled with the second person pronoun 'you' to allude an imagined reader. Where the style model's use of pronouns expresses bitterness at the universe, in my piece, the personalisation of 'I' in the simple declarative "I am gay" evokes the idea that I am proud of the statement. This is emphasised by the structure of a simple declarative with a single sentence paragraph, which might also serve to shock readers.

Letters can sometimes use rhetoric to influence readers and create effective writing. My style model for example uses figurative language to make points more striking because of the images and connotations they conjure: the metaphor "lit with sparks and laughter" achieves this by creating an image of the writer's feelings of excitement at the new relationship. I decided to use similar features like personification in "I don't know if these words will meet your loving eyes". By personifying my words, and the reader's 'eyes', the intended audience of my family will feel assured that this letter is not designed to cause pain, as evident in the attributive evaluative adjective 'loving'.

My style model uses a semantic field of competitiveness to create cohesion and intrigue; "game" and "cheated" semantically link to analogise the writers love-life as a fight for the best man, which lets the reader have insight to the writer's personal experiences of love. Similarly, I used a semantic field of musical theatre, a known passion of mine by the audience, in the form of an extended metaphor of performing throughout the letter, "My life slowly morphed into a musical of its own". This illustrates experiences that are presented in the letter in a more personal way, helping the audience to understand the specific experience of me pretending to be someone I am not. By using this rhetoric device, it entertains as well as making the point more interesting to read, engaging the audience leaving them wanting more of the story. My continuous use of lexis in this sematic field such as "acting", "script" and "curtain" acts as a cohesive device and creates a fluidity that binds the writing together.

Repetition is another rhetorical feature, stressing the most important words and creating a sense of rhythm. The writer in my style model repeats the past tense dynamic verb "waited" multiple times to emphasise her frustration at never meeting the right man. Similarly, I repeated the predicative evaluative adjective "scared" to emphasise the difficulty of this disclosure.

The use of the stative verb "love" in my style model indicates the intensity of feeling and emphasises the emotions of the writer. This inspired me to include my own stative verbs to devise an impactful paragraph using a compound sentence structure to include multiple clauses, all containing a stative verb of significance. The verbs appear in increasing intensity: "hope", "show", "teach", "prove". By ordering them this way, the audience read a crescendo of powerful desires which describe the intentions this letter has for me as the writer. I italicised these specific words to highlight the importance of them and my growing apprehension of the prospect of disclosure.

My style model mentions the idyllic future relationship using emotive language like "children" and "married". Emotive lexis has a greater emotional impact on the audience which is why I included the picture-perfect life I will never have in the form of emotive language. "White picket fences" and "perfect bride" are examples of materialistic desires parents often have for their children. By stating that I will never achieve these traditional goals, the audience will be able to understand why it is difficult to come out as you are breaking your parent's views on how your future will look.

This commentary scored 19/25.

Language Investigation

The language investigation is worth 10% of the A-Level and is marked out of 50. It assesses AO1, AO2 and AO3. The total length should be approximately 2000 words, excluding quotations.

You should consult with your teacher about the topic for your investigation but you should choose an area of language which you are interested in. This may come in many forms – here are a few examples:

- Political speech analysis
- Gendered speech in movie analysis
- Teenspeak investigation
- The language of adverts
- The language of TV presenters
- The language of TV psychics
- The language of Shakespeare

The options are endless!

Your investigation should be broken down into the following sections:

1. Introduction
Introduce the topic you are studying – mention some of the key theorists in this area which you will use later in the essay. Contextualise your research, also – let the examiner understand why you have chosen this area and the direction you will be taking it. You should also make a hypothesis – what do you expect to find out? **It should be approximately 250 words.**

2. Methodology
Describe how the data was collected. Be specific – for example, why did you choose that film? Why did you choose that speech? How did you ensure you were accurate in counting the use of intensifiers? Then, discuss how you get your data ready to be analysed. How did it go from just language to something you can analyse? **It should be approximately 250 words.**

3. Analysis

In this section, you will need to analyse your data. You can choose to format this how you wish, however, it is my strong suggestion that you use subheadings to organise your writing. It may be a good idea to use language levels as headings, though this is entirely up to you. One thing which may help you is to start by writing out a bullet-pointed list of conclusions you can draw from the data and from that, expanding each one. Each point should be supported with data (and if possible, a statistic) and a link to a theory. You should then explore whether that theory supports or refutes your data. In most cases, you will use a theory to explain your data. For example, 'the female characters used more intensifiers by 65%. Lakoff's theory supports this as her research details that overuse of intensifiers is a key area of women's language'. If this example were to be extended, it could link further data and perhaps challenge the findings by using a different theory. **It should be approximately 1250 words.**

4. Conclusion

The conclusion should summarise the main findings of the investigation and you should relate this to what you said in the introduction. You should also consider suggesting where further research could go and where you could improve your investigation (e.g. wider sample, more participants). **It should be approximately 250 words.**

Example Language Investigation

Introduction

Our ever-increasing dependence on our phones, laptops and social media has opened up a new realm of opportunity for political campaigning. Ever since its launch in 2004, Facebook has allowed companies to target particular socio-economic groups based on factors like gender, age, location and political viewpoint. It wasn't until the 2016 EU referendum when these were picked up for use as propaganda when the campaign 'Leave.EU' used these targeted adverts. Following this, in the 2017 general election, the Conservative party picked up this idea and adopted it by targeting voters in marginal constituencies to try and take the seat. Having a strong interest in the developing nature of politics and campaigning, this area marks a new and interesting area for investigation, and hopefully exploration of language use will prove exciting insights into the changing face of political advertising.

Aims

The main aim of the investigation is to examine how language is used to position the audience and how it is used to persuade voters to vote for their party, or how they are used to dissuade voters to vote for a particular party. The expectation is that Conservative adverts will focus on drilling into Labour policies or politicians (i.e. Jeremy Corbyn) rather than forming what Bakhtin describes as dialogic links between the adverts and their manifesto. This is because generally, it is easier to attack another party or their policies than it is to promote your policies. The Conservative campaign was fought on a 'who would be a better leader for Brexit? May or Corbyn?' stance, so it is expected that this will take a predominant role in the adverts. The Telegraph reported that The Conservatives were working with a "largely negative campaign strategy, targeting Jeremy Corbyn's 'weak leadership'" "[1]. A further aim to the investigation will be to look at the register of the adverts. The Conservatives are typically high register users when using the spoken mode, evident in many speeches, such as the launch of the manifesto speech, in which Theresa May uses strictly formal language. The investigation will look at whether The Conservatives converge downwards or diverge upwards in these adverts. The prediction is that there will be a slight convergence downwards in order to not be seen as aloof and distance voters.

Methodology

The research was collected by utilising news articles which focussed on the attack adverts. Without this resource, data collection would be limited due to the geographical and sociological targeting nature of the adverts, hence why videos have not been transcribed for analysis. To acknowledge copyright, these have all been credited with the source the article provides, and the website address of the article. The adverts were sampled and reduced from 15 adverts ranging from all political parties to 6 adverts focused on The Conservatives, to ensure language parallels to be drawn. By reducing the number of adverts, the reliability is also reduced due to the reducing view of the bigger picture. The Conservatives were contacted and asked to provide copies of their adverts, but did not respond to the request. The transcribed articles were combined to form a corpus, and a lexical analysis took place. A reductionist approach doesn't allow us to look at the words in the context of their independent adverts. For example, inductive coding allowed us to see the different ways the adverts engaged with the social and cultural contexts of the relevant socio-economic groups/geographical area. The use of Facebook as a platform for advertising is already a targeted approach, with the Facebook demographic being predominantly the younger members of society, with 68% of users being under 35.[2]

The analysis is a mix of quantitative and qualitative and was coded inductively so that generalisations are avoided until conclusions have been drawn from across all of the pieces, thus increasing internal validity. Due to the investigation being specialised to The Conservatives in the 2017 General Election, the research doesn't necessarily have external validity, and so couldn't be scaled out to attack adverts used in the US Election, or the EU referendum. The theories of audience positioning were applied, focusing on the research of Atkinson's political rhetoric and Fairclough's synthetic personalisation and power theories. In order to analyse the data inductively, the adverts were transcribed and collated into a corpus, which was alphabetised (see dataset 1). This allowed for patterns to be identified within the data as a whole without context.

Analysis: Lexis and semantics

An excerpt from figure 1.3: Top 18 words (excluding pronouns, conjunctions, numbers or prepositions)

Rank	Lexeme	Frequency	% of total words	No. different sources it appears in
1	Corbyn	13	5.1%	6
2	brexit	10	3.9%	4
3	risk	10	3.9%	4
4	Jeremy	8	3.1%	6
5	Theresa	7	2.7%	4
6	deal	6	2.3%	3
7	May	6	2.3%	4

The data shows, that despite the adverts being produced by The Conservatives, 'Corbyn' is the most frequent lexeme. What is particularly interesting, is that the adverts aren't attacking the opposition in terms of Labour, but instead attacking Jeremy Corbyn, seemingly using him as a metonym for Labour. Atkinson discusses the use of metaphors (and more broadly metonyms) as being rhetorical key devices. At the time, there was a stigma surrounding Jeremy Corbyn as a person, and a leader, with rivals discussing issues such as links with the IRA, and so perhaps he was seen as an easy target which could be used to defile 'The Labour Party'. Alternatively, The Conservatives may have opted to use Corbyn to not upset Labour supporters by lambasting their party. This can be evidenced when examining the context. For example, source 2 was found in the constituency of Bishop Auckland, which is a Labour stronghold, and has been a Labour seat since 1935[3]. In a similar way to the 'propaganda model', which states that the news "passes through five filters [which] ultimately shape[s] [what the] audiences receive"[4], the audience will filter political messages in a way which fits their own ideology[5]. In light of this, it's possible that Corbyn was used to bypass the filtering of Labour supporters, by attacking him instead of Labour, especially given the internal conflicts within Labour, which might suggest that the adverts are targeting anti-Corbyn Labourites.

Contrary to what was expected, there was very little of Fairclough's synthetic personalisation, with both second person singular and possessive pronouns ("you" and "your") getting 2 uses each. It is possible that being more collective in the adverts helps to create a sense of community. What was used more was the concrete noun "vote". Votes and voting are synonymous with democracy, something which the British government holds as a key British value[6]. The Conservatives are here adopting cultural beliefs into their adverts to play into patriotic values of the text receiver, by encouraging their democratic right to "vote". Holmes and Stubbe studied hierarchy and authority, and they found that those in higher ranks would downplay or assert authority. It's possible that the Conservatives are downplaying their authority, with the idea of the equality of power in voting, in the sense that everybody has the same level of power - a vote.

Something which occurred much higher than expected was the noun "risk". In figure 1.2, it had 10 instances within the 6 sources. From this, further analysis was taken into fearmongering in the adverts, examining risk, its hyponyms and linked clauses:

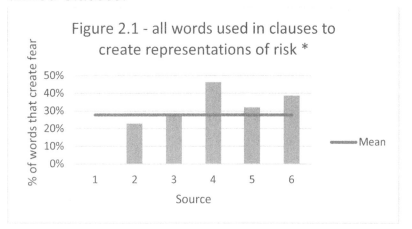

Figure 2.1 - all words used in clauses to create representations of risk *

*Clauses were chosen at personal discretion of what 'risk' counts as.

The graph shows us that on average, 28% of all the words used evokes meanings of fear and risk. Looking at figure 2.1, it's clear that source 1 is anomalous, due to it having 0 words directly relating to fear. This is probably because source 1 is just a picture, without a caption, unlike the other 5 sources. To increase reliability, if the investigation were to be repeated, a source which has a caption should produce more accurate results. In order to consider the data more accurately, figure 2.2 shows the data excluding source 1.

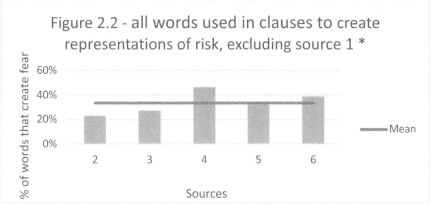

Figure 2.2 - all words used in clauses to create representations of risk, excluding source 1 *

*Clauses were chosen at personal discretion of what 'risk' counts as.

The graph shows that on average, over a third (34%) of the words used within the adverts has the purpose of inciting and instilling fear within the text receiver. For example, in source 2, it says "There's so much at stake", with the adverbial intensifier "so" escalating the situation, almost hyperbolically. However, the advert doesn't do is explain what the "so much" is. This allows them to make these sweeping statements with no evidence to support their claim. It's possible that this is to create power. Fairclough has discussed the principal of power in and behind the discourse, the advert having a strong message of risk whilst the receiver is reading the text, with the idea being that the fear will remain with the reader after they have read it. They are positioning themselves as the 'saviour' type option by revealing the consequences of voting for Labour.

Pragmatics

When the texts are examined pragmatically, we start to see other patterns and complexities arising. What's particularly interesting is how the adverts tend to tap more into the cultural context of patriotism, than a social context, although it could be argued that the rise in overt patriotism is a social context in itself. For example, source 3 and 4 talk about "our nation" and "our Brexit deal" with the use of the third person collective possessive plural pronoun designed to encourage a sense of national identity and pride. Holmes and Stubbe's research would suggest that the use of "our" positions the Conservatives as amongst the readers and voters as it reduces the social distance between them. However, there is instances of the adverts using the social context, for example, source 2 talks about the impact of taxes on "working families". Historically, Labour are the party of the working class, but instead, The Conservatives have decided to selectively adopt this element to appeal to the social makeup of the voters. They are appealing to the idea that Labour are failing their core audience, and so are targeting the voters who the Conservatives usually ignore. In Source 2's Bishop Auckland placing, earnings are significantly below that of the national average[6], so it's clear to see that these adverts are targeting key social issues for voters.

When considering the aims of the investigation, it was proposed that the adverts would converge downwards, however, there isn't conclusive evidence to suggest converging formality within the adverts. The adverts remain largely formal, with the occasional lapse, in terms of contractions. Through keeping the formality, they keep their overt prestige associated with Standard English. There is, however, a sense of idiomatic usage within the adverts, with the intensified adverbs in phrases such as "so much at stake" in source 2, and "just not up to the job" in source 3. This said, they do not detract from the core message of the adverts, mainly because they are positioned after the key point in a different paragraph. It's possible that it acts as a structural device of ensuring the message is accessible to all.

Discourse

In terms of cohesion, the adverts' rhetorical purpose naturally leads to a cohesive piece. Lexical cohesion is created by various different forms of repetition, such as use of hypozeuxis in source 1, which describes the construction of each of the declaratives having its own subject and verb, for example "can't negotiate" and "won't negotiate", designed to deceive the text receivers into thinking that they are making separate arguments, despite making the same argument with 3 strands of evidence. In addition, there is the use of parison with the matching patterns across the triadic structure of "Brexit deal". Atkinson discusses the use of repetition, particularly in association with triads, as being a core principal political rhetoric. The use of repetition of key messages, like "Brexit deal", acts as a mental highlighter for the reader. Atkinson's research detailed that usually in speeches, the third item generated applause. In a similar way, source 1 adopts a problem-solution structure within the triad with the first 2 sentences creating the problem of Labour ("can't") or the Liberal Democrats ("won't") negotiating a Brexit deal and the third offering the reprieve of Theresa May ("can").

Graphology

Traditionally, The Conservatives and the colour blue are strong collocates, likewise, Labour and red, however, in the sources, blue is only present in 2 of the adverts. As with the language, the adverts are visually centred on Labour. With the context of the adverts being placed on Facebook, they need to be eye-catching so that users will stop and read the adverts, whilst scrolling down their newsfeed. With red being omnipresent in the adverts, they will look, to the average person not paying much attention to what the text is saying, like a Labour advert. This is particularly useful when considering adverts placed in Labour strongholds, as the adverts are subverting the power of Labour. On average, consumers spent 2 seconds looking at or reading an advert in print before they decide to read it or not[7]. Considering that 80% of usage comes from smartphones[8], where a user can very quickly scroll past anything they're not interested in, these adverts need to catch the eye of the user almost immediately.

In addition to using colour, source 3 opts to use grammatically non-standard features, by orthographically manipulating the case of the opening clause, "MUST WATCH". This immediately accentuates the advert to the reader, draws their attention and then gives them instruction, via the modal auxiliary imperative "must". In fact, the phrase has a sense of 'we're helping you out by showing you this', as if they are selflessly aiding the public in their voting decision. Holmes and Stubbe studied hierarchy and authority, and they found that those in higher ranks would downplay or assert authority. In terms of the advert, The Conservatives are downplaying their authority by being non-standard to appeal to the voters as being 'down to Earth' and not aloof.

Conclusion

When considering the data holistically and inductively, clear patterns and their complexities emerge. The research could have been done with deductive coding, but this limits the reliability of the research, as a particular feature may only occur once in the data set, but appear in numerous other adverts. It can be concluded that the Conservative Party's adverts had a strong focus on Labour as the opposition, Jeremy Corbyn, and their policies, rather than promoting their own figure heads and policies. The lexical analysis particularly accentuates this. Furthermore, the adverts have been designed to be aesthetically similar to the adverts of the Labour Party, to attract the attention of Labour voters. This is particularly pertinent when considering that these adverts are targeting specific demographics, usually in Labour strongholds. With the adverts sourced from the social media sphere in which users are presented with multiple different posts and adverts, the unsuspecting Facebook user may think that this is an advert for their party.

Should the investigation be completed again, a wider range of sources should be used which cover a larger range of the political spectrum, to compare whether language use was consistent or individual across parties. Also, the validity could have been improved by gathering the sources directly, rather than relying on an online collection, but this is difficult to do, as Facebook will only show adverts that are targeted in the geographically and socially relevant for the user. There is also the issue of the appellation of meaning. The lexis analysis was based on the meaning that was placed on the adverts from personal discretion on what is classed as a 'risk' word, which could potentially alter how the adverts are read.

This piece scored 50/50.

Wider reading list

One way to improve your knowledge is by reading around the subject. Here is a selection of wider reading resources which may help you to improve your knowledge.

General Language:
- *A Little Book of Language* by David Crystal
- Anything written by Dan Clayton (including his blog). He is on Twitter @EngLangBlog.
- *The English Language* by David Crystal
- *How Language Works* by David Crystal
- Cambridge Topics in English Language

Language diversity:
- *The Myth of Mars and Venus: Do Men and Women Really Speak Different Languages?* By Deborah Cameron.
- *Sociolinguistics: An Introduction to Language and Society* by Peter Trudgill
- *Through the Language Glass* by Guy Deutscher
- *The Prodigal Tongue* by Lynne Murphy
- *You Say Potato* by David Crystal
- *Language Attitudes* by Dan Clayton
- *Language Diversity and World Englishes* by Dan Clayton and Rob Drummond

Language change:
- *The Adventure of English* (book and documentary) by Melvyn Bragg.
- *The Stories of English* by David Crystal
- *The Gr8 Deb8* by David Crystal
- *Language Change* by Ian Cushing

Language acquisition:
- *Listen to your Child* by David Crystal
- *Child Language* by Matthew Saxton
- *Language Development* by Rachel Rudman

Glossary

Accent – how you say something.

Acronymisation and initialisation – taking the first letters in phrases and forming a word.

Acronyms - words formed based on its initials but can be said as a word.

Addition – the child adds something completely new into the pronunciation.

Adjacency pairs - pairs of conventional pieces of speech – the speaker will say one and the hearer will reply in a specific way.

Adjective – a word which is a description.

Adverb – a word which modifies a verb.

Affixation – adding a prefix to an existing word.

Affricate – starts as an affricate and ends as a plosive.

Alveolar – the tongue is placed just behind the teeth on the alveolar ridge.

Amelioration – a word gains a more positive meaning.

Anaphoric – references which look back.

Antonym – a word with the opposite meaning.

Approximant – parts of the mouth are brought together but do not touch.

Archaic – old and out-dated.

Assimilation – the child uses a sound from earlier or later in the word as it is easier to say.

Babbling – production of syllable sounds.

Back-channelling – where a speaker passively agrees with what's being said.

Behaviourism – the belief that a child learns to speak through positive and negative reinforcement.

Bilabial – both lips are used.

Bleaching – a word loses power.

Blending – taking parts of two existing words.

Borrowing/loan words – new words are brought in from other languages.

Brummie – speakers who using a Birmingham accent.

Caregiver – a person who supports a child.

Cataphoric – references which look forward.

Clipping or abbreviating – removing part of a word.

Code – a form of language.

Codification – the process by which a change becomes official.

Collocation/collocates – words which go together.

Complex sentence – a sentence which contains at least one subordinate clause.

Compound sentence – two or more simple sentences joined by a conjunction.

Compounding – combining two existing words.

Conjunction - a word which combines clauses.

Connotation – the associated ideas with a word.

Consonant cluster reduction – the child removes some consonant sounds from the word.

Contraction – removal of parts of a word, usually replaced with an apostrophe.

Convergence – language becomes more similar.

Conversationalisation – the process by which conversations become more and more informal.

Conversion – a word changes class.

Cooing – the baby makes sounds.

Covert prestige – a form of social value you get from using non-standard forms.

Cursive – joining up letters when writing.

Declarative – used to make statement.

Deixis – a word which is only understood in context.

Deletion – the child removes from the word altogether.

Denotation – dictionary definition.

Dental – the tongue is on the teeth.

Derogation – a word gets a worse meaning over time.

Descriptivism – belief that all language varieties are positive.

Determiner – a word which modifies a noun.

Dialect – the words you use.

Digraph – two letters.

Diminutive – addition of a morpheme which relates to making the thing smaller. Usually used by parents and children by adding a <y> to the end of words.

Diphthongs – a sound which is a glide – the mouth has to move to accommodate it.

Discourse structure – the way a text is structured.

Divergence – language becomes more different.

Dysphemism – a blunt way of saying thing.

Echoing – repeating what the child says.

Elaborated code – a way of speaking which is clear and understandable.

Eponymisation – using someone's name to form a word.

Ethnolect – the language of an ethnic group.

Euphemism – a less harsh way of saying things.

Exclamative – used to make an exclamation.

Expansion – a word's definition expands to cover more.

Expansion – repeating what the child said, but in a more linguistically sophisticated way.

Expatiation – repeating what the child said but adding more information.

Expletives – swear words.

Face – personal and social value a person has or thinks they have.

Face-threatening act – an act which attacks someone's freedom or feelings.

False starts – the speaker starts to speak and then stops and retries that start.

Fatherese – the way fathers speak to their children.

Filler – words which the speaker uses to gain time to think.

Fricative – push of air.

G-dropping – the word-final /g/ sound gets dropped.

Genderlect – the language of a gender.

Glottal – produced in the glottis (in the throat).

Glottal stop – the missing out of the /t/ sound in words.

Grammar – the study of how language is structured.

Grapheme – letters.

Grapheme-Phoneme Correspondence – where the sounds match with the letters.

Graphemic cluster omission – a cluster of letters has been omitted from the word.

Graphemic cluster substitution – a cluster of letters has been substituted for another set.

H-dropping – the word-initial /h/ sound gets dropped.

Hedging – phrases which express weak opinion.

Hierarchy – the structure of power within an institution

Holophrase – a single word.

Hypernym – an umbrella/generic term.

Hyponym – a part of a larger collection.

Hypotaxis – joining clauses using subordination.

Imperative – used to make a command.

Inference – a meaning which has been deduced.

Inflection – a morpheme which is added to a word to change it.

Initialisms – words formed based on its initials.

Inkhorn terms – terms borrowed from Greek and Latin during the Renaissance.

Insertion – a (spurious) letter is added which does not belong in the word.

Intensifiers – words which increase the meaning or value of a word.

Interactionalism – the belief that a child learns to speak through interaction with others.

Interrogative – used to ask a question.

Intonation – the rising and falling of the voice.

Irregular verb – a verb which does not take an inflection to change the tense.

Jargon – language used which is specific to a certain area.

Labelling - providing the label.

Labiodental – combines the lips and teeth.

LAD – the Language Acquisition Device – an inbuilt device which helps children to learn language.

LASS – the Language Acquisition Support System – the way caregivers scaffold language to help children.

Lateral – air goes past the side of the tongue.

Legalese – the language of law. A highly Latinate language and often very opaque to non-legal workers.

Lexical innovation – using words we already have to form new ones

Lexical invention – using completely new words.

Lexis – the study of words.

Magic e – the <e> at the end of words which is silent.

Main clause (also called independent clause) – the core of the sentence – can exist on its own.

Manner of articulation – the way in which a word is articulated.

Matched guise – an experiment where one speaker speaks in a range of different accents in order for people to pass a judgement about an accent.

Melodic utterances – utterances which have a sense of rhythm or intonation.

Minor/fragment – an incomplete sentence (missing one or more of SVO).

MKO – More Knowledgeable Other – a person who fills a child's ZPD.

MLE – Multicultural London English – an ethnolect/sociolect which originates from Black speakers in London.

Monophthongs – a single sound – the mouth stays in one place to articulate it.

Morpheme – the smallest unit of meaning.

Motherese – the way mothers speak to their children.

Multiple negation – using more than one negative in a sentence.

Nasal – uses the nose.

Nativism – the belief that there is something innate in children which helps them to learn language.

Negative reinforcement – punishing behaviour in the hope it won't be repeated.

Neologisation – a completely new word is invented.

Neosemy – a word gains a completely new meaning.

Non-fluency features – features which disrupt the flow of conversation.

Noun – a word which is a person, place or thing.

Numerical-phonetic substitution – substitution of numbers to represent phonetic sounds.

Object permeance – the idea that things exist when you don't see them.

Omission – a letter is missed from the word which should be there.

Orthographic manipulation – changing the norms for writing.

Orthography – the study of writing.

Otherese – the way people speak to children.

Over-articulation - elongating vowel sounds.

Overt prestige – a form of social value you get from using standard forms.

Palatal – the tongue is on the roof of the mouth.

Parataxis – simple sentences joined with no conjunctions or coordinating conjunctions.

Parenthetical clause – a clause which exists in brackets.

Phatic conversation – conversation which fulfils a social function. Sometimes called small talk.

Phoneme – a sound.

Phonemic contraction – the baby only uses phonemes from its own language.

Phonemic expansion – the baby explores the phonemes it can produce.

Phonic approach – used to help children read aloud – children are encouraged to spell out the word by recognising what graphemes, digraphs and trigraphs correspond to what phonemes.

Phonology – the study of sounds and the production of sounds.

Phrases – words around a head word.

Place of articulation – the place in which a word is articulated.

Plosive – quick start and stop of air.

Polari – a secret code used by gay men to communicate when homosexuality was illegal.

Political correctness – avoiding language which could be deemed offensive.

Positive reinforcement – encouraging behaviour in the hope it will be repeated.

Post-alveolar – the tongue is slightly further back from the alveolar ridge.

Post-modification – adjectives which come after the noun.

Post-telegraphic stage – the child produces complex utterances.

Poverty of stimulus – caregivers provide a poor examine of language.

Pragmatics – the study of implied meaning.

Pre-modification – adjectives which come before the noun.

Prefix – a morpheme which is added to the start of a word.

Preposition – a word which indicates a position.

Prescriptivism – belief that language should be prevented from changing.

Pronoun – a word which indicates a person.

Protowords – made-up 'words' attached to things.

Psycholinguistic approach – used to help children to read – they are encouraged to decode words based on their context.

Received Pronunciation (RP) – an accent which is typically described as 'posh' – it uses all the prestigious pronunciations. Its association with the Queen and the BBC leads it to be viewed as 'correct'.

Reduplicated babbling – repeating the same sound.

Reduplication – combining two similar sounds.

Reformulation – repeating what the child says, but in a different way.

Relative clause – a clause which adds more information and is introduced by a relative pronoun.

Repair – the speaker makes a mistake and then corrects it.

Restricted code – a way of speaking which masks meaning and is inherently deictic.

Restriction – a word loses some of its meanings.

Rhotic accent – pronounces the 'r' after vowels in words like 'car'.

Schema – a knowledge structure.

Semantic field – a group of words/phrases with a common meaning.

Semantics – the study of meaning.

Shibboleth – a collection of features based on how language is used in a place.

Simple sentence – a main clause on its own.

Sociolect – the language of a social group.

Standard forms – the socially accepted way of saying things (using Standard English).

Strong verbs – verbs which change when changing the tense.

Subordinate clause (also called dependant clause) – exists as an addition to the main clause – it cannot exist without it.

Substitution – the child substitutes an easier phoneme in place of an easier one.

Suffix – a morpheme which is added to the end of a word.

Synonym – a word with the same meaning.

Syntax – word order.

Teenspeak – the language of teenagers.

Telegraphic stage – the child produces utterances with just enough words to make sense.

TH-fronting – pronouncing the 'th' at the start of words as /f/.

Transposed letters – a letter has been written the wrong way round.

Trigraph – three letters.

Turn taking – where speakers take turns to speak

Two-word stage – the child produces two-word utterances.

Universal grammar – the idea that every child has an understanding of grammar built into their brain.

Variegated babbling – repeating different sounds.

Velar – the tongue is pressed against the back of the mouth.

Verb – a word which describes an action.

Virtuous error – an error which is made but it is clear how the child has made the mistake.

Weak verbs – verbs which take an inflection when changing tense.

Whole-word approach – used to help children to read – they are encouraged to look and say. It relies on children memorising large numbers of words

Yod-coalescence – the pronunciation of the /j/ sound in words like Tuesday.

ZPD – Zone of Proximal Development – a gap of knowledge.

Addition theories or vocabulary

Use these pages to add in age extra theories or vocabulary which you may know but aren't in this book:

Printed in Great Britain
by Amazon

16371361R00081